EACH CENTERED PERSON BECOMES AN OWNER, NOT A RENTER OF KNOWLEDGE. CENTER YOURSELF.

Molefi Kete Asante

i

Certain conventions are used in Asante Imprint Books to avoid biased or sexist language, for consistency and accessibility, or to reflect the Afrocentric philosophy of *Asante Imprint Books*.
Some of these conventions are:
- B.C.E. for Before the Common Era, instead of B.C.
- C.E. for Common Era, instead of A.D.
- Treatment of oral history and prehistory as equal with written history.
- Spellings of ancient gods and certain names are transliterated from the hieroglyphs in closer form to their original African presentation.
- Selected ancient country and city names used are the ancient African names rather than the Greek or Roman versions.

Photo Credits: pp.8, 11, 12, 14, 47, 54, 57, 59, 61, 72, 73, 79, 82, 83, 94, 98, 107, 114, 118, 124, 129, 135, 139, Pencil Point Studios; p.18, British Museum; Archives; pp. 27, 28, 43, 44, 55, 58, 73, 76, 77, 86, 96, 111, 125, Jocelyn Chu, Illustrator; pp.53, 95, 97, 116, 123, 124, 128, Courtesy of Anheuse Co.; p.68, C Clymer; pp.71, 85, PPG File Photo; p.74, AP/Wide World; p.80, Jerry Tadden National Museum of African Art, Eliot Elisonfon Archives, Smithsonian Institution; p.133, Courtesy of Freer Gallery of Art, Smithsonian Institution; p.140, Jeffery Polskonka, National Museum of African Art, Eliot Elisonfon Archives Smithsonian Institution. All other photos are from Dr. Asante's Archives.

Photo research by Daniel Ortiz, Jr.

ISBN 1-56256-900-7

10 9

ASANTE

CLASSICAL AFRICA

by

Dr. Molefi Kete Asante

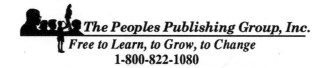

The Peoples Publishing Group, Inc.
Free to Learn, to Grow, to Change
1-800-822-1080

ASANTE

INTRODUCTION TO THE ASANTE IMPRINT BOOKS
BY DR. MOLEFI KETE ASANTE

A story is told in Africa of a man and a woman who traversed all of central Africa in search of a particular waterfall. After a long, arduous journey through desert, swamp, and rain forest, they finally came to the waterfall they sought. The beauty of the waterfall in the heart of Africa was stunning, surpassing everything they had imagined. The man and the woman looked at each other and said, **"At last!"** It was both a sigh of relief at finally completing their difficult journey and an expression of joy at the beauty of the final outcome.

At last we have the first declared Afrocentric series of books for students in our schools, the *Asante Imprint Books*.

Asante Imprint Books, published by the Peoples Publishing Group, are a profoundly Afrocentric endeavor. Many publishers have offered watered-down versions of multiculturalism in textbooks; others have attempted to inject African and African American people and information as sidebars, pop-up features, and highlighted or marginal elements in the standard curriculum. Still other publishers have been afraid to even use the perfectly good word *Afrocentric. Do not confuse Asante Imprint Books, published by the Peoples Publishing Group, with those other watered-down books.*

By Afrocentric, I mean that the African American person is placed in the center of each book, and that each *Asante Imprint Book* is written from within an African-centered perspective. For the first time, teachers using *Asante Imprint Books* will have materials that allow them to center themselves and their students within the culture, history, and

experiences of African centeredness. *Asante Imprint Books* put any reader of any age on-line with the centric idea.

To examine culture, history, and other fields from one center within that field is a natural enough inclination for any student. The same sense of centeredness must be given to the person of African descent as to other cultures.

Centeredness seems to me to be a simple concept in any intellectual enterprise, and Afrocentricity is an intellectual philosophy which I first propounded and defined in 1980. For my colleagues and myself, the *Asante Imprint Books* represent the first time that a serious publisher, the *Peoples Publishing Group, Inc.,* has sought out the experts, created the opportunity, and provided schools and individuals with books that incorporate African centeredness.

In the *Asante Imprint Books,* Afrocentricity means that the African American is viewed as a agent, an actor in the story of history, rather than a passive observer on the sidelines. To teach with an Afrocentric approach means to find the African agency in any given presentation of history, culture, literature, or other field. It means helping students discover how active the African person or idea is in a given situation, narrative, illustration, or example. In other words, you are learning and teaching from the perspective or standpoint of the African person. To find agency and center your students, of course, means seeing the agency of all students when you present information about their cultures, histories and experiences. The *Asante Imprint Books* were created to be the first Afrocentric school materials, and the books were designed carefully to place students in an African center.

ASANTE

To accomplish our Afrocentric goal, you will find six clearly articulated elements in all *Asante Imprint Books*.

First, *Asante Imprint Books* give students or readers a sense of ownership of knowledge by centering them in the middle of the information rather than consigning them to the margins as mere renters of someone else's information.

Second, *Asante Imprint Books* view people of African descent as major actors in human history, not as observers on the sidelines. In this regard, you will note that the language is carefully written to avoid dehumanizing any group of people and, instead, to make the story of history a personal and holistic experience. Rather than referring to "African slaves," we refer to "enslaved people" and strive to give countries of origin and identify real people whenever possible. Similarly, we are careful to keep the language as Afrocentric as possible, choosing to refer to countries, cities, groups of people, gods, and individuals by African spellings of their proper names rather than names given to them by the West or by Greece or Rome. For example, we take care to explain to students that ancient Egypt was called *Kemet* by the African people who lived there. And we encourage students to evaluate the use of words with Western denotations, such as *classical,* which too often implies a Greek or Roman standard to the exclusion of all other cultures as though others were inferior.

Third, *Asante Imprint Books* clearly identify scholarly information that is the result of current research, archaeology, discoveries, and academic thinking

ASANTE

about Africa and African Americans. An icon with the continent of Africa on it identifies this new, distinctly Afrocentric information.

Four, *Asante Imprint Books* emphasize holistic learning rather than one-dimensional learning. Students are challenged not only to learn new facts, but to extend their knowledge to intellectual and emotional levels. History becomes personal as students become centered in the culture and draw their own lessons from it. An icon with four African people on it identifies passages that demand holistic learning.

Fifth, *Asante Imprint Books* are distinguished in their scholarship. I am senior author on all *Asante Imprint Books,* and each book is written by scholars and educators who are both expert and current in their respective fields. This means that *Asante Imprint Books* are historically and culturally accurate, as well as up-to-date.

Sixth, all *Asante Imprint Books* have the Asante instructional design. All questions and activities reinforce the Asante philosophy. For example, at the end of every unit, a **Personal Witnessing** activity directs students to first reflect individually on their new holistic knowledge, and then to share their testimony of what they have learned personally with the class.

The Asante instructional design combines Afrocentric and holistic learning in centering questions and activities never before presented in any textbook. Teachers and curriculum experts will appreciate the elegance of the Asante instructional design.

ASANTE

I personally encourage administrators, teachers, and parents to use *Asante Imprint Books* to the advantage of their students. *Asante Imprint Books* may be used in any region of the world with any student.

Hopefully, like the travellers in my opening paragraph, you, too, will exclaim upon receiving the *Asante Imprint Books,* **"At last!"**

Dr. Molefi Kete Asante

Dr. Molefi Kete Asante, Senior Author, is Professor and Chair, Department of African American Studies, Temple University, Philadelphia, Pennsylvania. He is among the leading Afrocentric educational consultants and scholars in the United States. Dr. Asante has authored more than thirty books related to Afrocentricity, and is considered by many scholars to be the Father of Afrocentricity for defining the term in his book **Kemet, Afrocentricity, and Knowledge.** *Dr. Asante is also an educational consultant for several school districts, including Washington, D.C.; Cleveland; Detroit; Indianapolis; Gary, Indiana; and Baltimore. His work with the schools demonstrates his "actvitist-scholar" philosophy.*

Dr. Judylynn Bailey-Mitchell, Ed. D., is the creator of all Questions and Instructional Activities for the Asante Imprint Books. Dr. Mitchell is a Vice Principal in the Wicomico County, Maryland, Public School District.

ASANTE

CLASSICAL AFRICA

TABLE OF CONTENTS

UNIT 1

"Egypt is to Africa and African people as Greece is to Europe and European people."

— **Cheikh Anta Diop**

AFRICA: THE EARLY CIVILIZATIONS

Africa is the birthplace of the human race. The earliest civilizations in Africa probably lived along the Nile River. Classical traditions refer to those ideas, art forms, and attitudes that are worthy of being considered models for others to follow.

CENTER YOURSELF

Africans in the United States come from the same continent as the ancient empires along the Nile River. What traits, qualities, or characteristics of contemporary Africans would you compare with the ancient civilizations along the Nile River?

The Great Sphinx and the Great Pyramid represent classical African art and attitudes.

The six classical civilizations of ancient Africa left a rich heritage
for the later civilizations of Greece and Rome and for the world today.

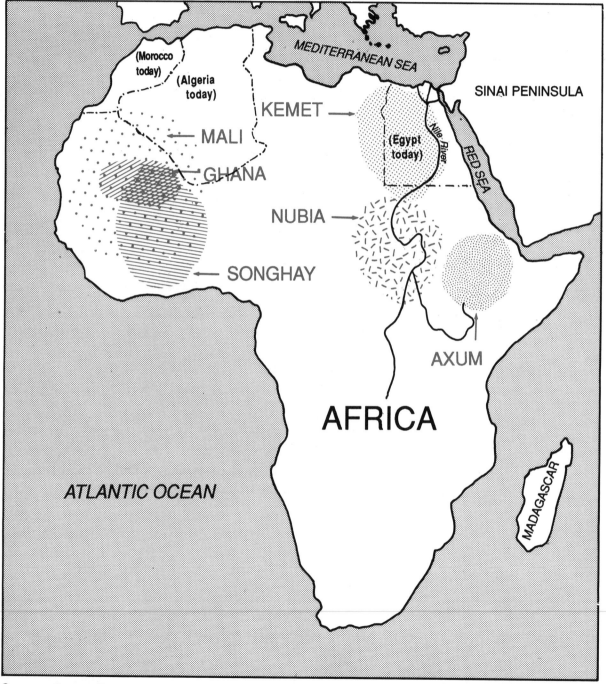

CHAPTER

1 AFRICAN BEGINNINGS

THE AFRICAN CONTINENT

Africa is the second largest continent. The only continent that is larger is Asia. There are 12 million square miles of land on the African continent. This means that the 48 states of the continental United States can fit comfortably into Africa five times.

 Size is not the only physical fact that may surprise you about the geography of the continent of Africa. Africa's many different types of land and climates also reflects its diversity. Think of all the different kinds of lands you know about, and you will have some idea of the many geographical differences in the land of Africa.

People who live in the upper midwest and northeast of the United States could say that Africa is not as cold as the regions in which they live. In most cases, they would be right because most of Africa is in the tropical or subtropical zones.

However, Africa also has vast deserts, mountain ranges, forests, and savanna regions. Some areas of the deserts have oases; other areas are uninhabited. There are mountains with snow caps and hills covered with palms.

Africa also has a rain forest which gets nearly 200 inches of rain each year. Think of snowfall in states such as Colorado and you have some idea of the amount of precipitation in Africa's rain forest.

▲ The great pyramids were built during the ancient classical season.

THE THREE SEASONS OF CLASSICAL AFRICA

There are three primary periods of African classical history, which I call *seasons*.

- The first season is from 6000 B.C.E. to 525 B.C.E, and I call it the *ancient classical season*.
- The second season begins around 525 B.C.E. and lasts until 641 C.E. I call it the *second classical season*.
- The third season is dated from 641 C.E. to 1600 C.E. I call it the *third classical season*.

THE ANCIENT CLASSICAL SEASON 6000 B.C.E. - 525 B.C.E.

The ancient classical season in Africa is the longest classical period in human history. It extends from the period of earliest settlements around the modern city of Khartoum and is dated from 6000 B.C.E. to 525 B.C.E.

During the ancient classical season, African traditions for kings, queens, and military leaders were established. The rituals and practices of many different African religions were created and consolidated. The great pyramids were built in

6000 B.C.E.		525 B.C.E	641 C.E.	1600 C.E.
First Classical Season		Second Classical Season	Third Classical Season	

Nubia and Kemet. Kemet was the name of ancient Egypt before the Greeks came and changed its name to *Aigyptos*, Egypt, meaning the "temples of Ptah." Art forms such as music, dance, and sculpture became standardized so that whatever came after looked something like what was created in this period.

Traditions developed during this period were emulated by succeeding generations as classical. Oral stories and traditions that had been reported and retold for hundreds of years became standardized as classical, influencing future generations down through today. In fact, the ancient classical season is the basis of behavioral and intellectual ideas and a source of inspiration for the seasons that followed. And, in this way, the classical season is alive in Africans and African Americans today.

THE SECOND CLASSICAL SEASON 525 C.E. - 641 C.E.

Classical African traditions and knowledge of the arts, sciences, and mathematics spread to the outside world during the second classical season. Other peoples learned more about the arts, sciences, and mathematics of Africa during this period. Partly, knowledge of African achievements spread because this period was one of instability for Africa.

Persia (which is now called Iran), Greece, and Syria became interested in African ideas and knowledge after they invaded Africa. The invasion of Egypt by the Persians and later the Greeks during this second season brought great change to Africa. Knowledge from Africa traveled back to Greece and Persia with the Greek and Persian students who went to Egypt to study. They went to Egypt because it was the oldest country known to human beings at the time.

Great Greek students, such as Plato, Isocrates, Pythagoras, and Homer studied with equally great African minds, such as Wennofer, Kagemni, Sonchis, and Khun-anup, who based their knowledge on the thousands of years of study and observation of their African ancestors.

Although outstanding changes and the sharing of knowledge were happening during this season, it was also a time of great instability. The African continent was invaded again and again.

▼ Ancient Persia invaded Egypt, gaining Egyptian ideas, advances, and knowledge.

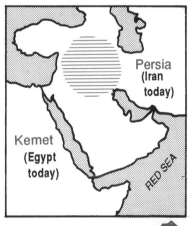

6000 B.C.E.

525 C.E.   641 C.E.   1600 C.E.

First Classical Season	Second Classical Season	Third Classical Season

First came the Persians and the Greeks; then came the Romans in 50 B.C.E. and, finally, the Arabs in 639-641 C.E. Egypt would never be the same again. The classical religions of the ancestors were shattered, and the language of the Egyptian people was supplanted by Arabic. Many of the customs changed. The government was controlled by an elite group of people who did not even live in Egypt. The Egyptian people were left with their classical traditions, their pyramids, tombs and temples, and the vast knowledge they had given to the world.

THE THIRD CLASSICAL SEASON 641 - 1600 C.E.

After the Arabs conquered northern Africa in the 7th century C.E., they unleashed a force that would have a powerful impact on all of northern Africa — the religion of Islam. Africa's third classical season is marked by the introduction of Islam into Africa.

Jihads, Islamic religious wars, were fought to convert Africans to the religion of the Arabs. Some Africans became followers of the religion and converted their neighbors to these new ideas.

From the 7th to the 9th century C.E., much of Africa was in a state of feverish activity. Africans were both rejecting and converting to new modes of thinking, while resisting military conquests. Schools were set up, scholars debated issues of significance, and travelers visited places they had never seen before.

The Arabs on the east and the Europeans on the north became the greatest threats to the safety and security of the African people. Africans were prized because of their strength, intelligence, and skills. They were enslaved and indentured and used as soldiers, farmers, fishers, blacksmiths, medical advisers, and teachers in Asia and the Americas.

The third classical season was also a time of some of the greatest African empires — Ghana, Mali, and Songhay. These great, classical empires will be presented in their own chapters later in this book.

6000 B.C.E.		525 C.E.	641 C.E.	1600 C.E.
	First Classical Season		Second Classical Season	Third Classical Season

1. What are the three primary seasons of classical Africa? Give the dates for each season. Tell one contribution from each season.

2. Compare the second and third classical seasons of Africa. Explain the changes that occurred in each season to threaten the stability of Africa.

3. **CRITICAL THINKING:** Reread your answer to question 2. Explain how the changes you described made the rest of the world aware of the knowledge, contributions, and ideas of Africa.

CHAPTER 2 THE NILE RIVER

VOCABULARY
Inundation   Emergence
Drought

CENTER YOUR VOCABULARY
civilization

THE LIFE-GIVING NILE

Without the Nile River, the earliest major civilization would probably not have grown up in Egypt. The Nile created the perfect setting for a rich civilization to flourish. No wonder some ancient Africans connected the Nile and its seasonal flooding with their religion and gods.

The Nile River is the longest river in the world. It starts almost at the center of the African continent and runs down toward the Mediterranean Sea, fanning out into a delta for a total distance of 6,737 kilometers (4,187 miles). The Delta is formed by the rich soil left by the river as it empties into the sea. Some of the earliest civilizations grew up along the Nile, communities of people who were advanced enough to live together without killing each other or being killed by their environment.

Both the longest river and the largest desert in the world are located on the continent of Africa. Both have had a profound effect on the lives and thinking of Africans.

An ancient Egyptian hymn says,

Hail to you,

O Nile,

that springs out of the earth

and comes to give life to Egypt!

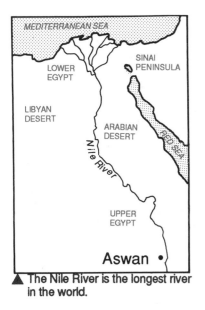

▲ The Nile River is the longest river in the world.

The banks of the Nile are lush with life, but the Nile also runs through the largest desert in the world. ▶

To the ancient Africans, the Nile River was mysterious and a force to be worshiped. The Nile was respected as the god, Hapi.

The Nile gave its abundant gifts to the earliest settlers along its banks. Here on either side of the river, the villages and towns that would give Africa its earliest organized civilization grew up. Other river valleys and regions on the continent would be important in the years to come, but it was the Nile above all that set the tone for African civilization. Along the Nile, the African civilization grew up. Along the Nile, the African people developed civilized ways to live together in peace.

The Nile overflowed its banks every year beginning in June. The people called this the Inundation.

When the waters matched their peak in September and began to recede, the people called the

▲ A boat on the Nile River today.

new season the Emergence. This period lasted until February, when there would be Drought until the waters began to rise at Inundation in June. Each year was the same.

During the Emergence, the Egyptians trapped water in ponds and also in humanmade lakes to use later for irrigation of their crops. They planted seeds in the rich soil left by the river. During the Inundation, the king employed farmers as artisans and builders.

Measurement experts monitored the water level of the river. They were the first people to provide detailed information on the rising of flood waters. They could tell by the height of the river upstream how high the flood waters would rise downstream. The experts in Aswan even knew exactly what height the waters would be near Abydos at a certain date.

As you can see, a lot depended on the precision of the experts. If the waters did not rise high enough, the farmers would have to carry water from the Nile in buckets to their farms. That could be a lot of buckets! But if you were smart and had planned to carry enough buckets, you would be able to get enough water from the river to your farm. You could survive a season of low water or drought.

In 1970, the Egyptian government completed the building of the Aswan High Dam after many years of trying to control the floodwaters. When water is needed, it is released from the dam. The water then enters a series of canals and lakes and flows to the farms to irrigate them.

CENTER YOUR THINKING

1. Using information from this chapter, draw your own picture of the Nile showing the Delta region as it empties into the Mediterranean Sea.

2. What specific skills did ancient measurement experts need to monitor the height of the Nile?

3. **CRITICAL THINKING:** Write your own poem of one verse about the Nile River. Consider in your poem the meaning and significance of the Nile to the ancient people in northeastern Africa who depended upon it for so much.

CHAPTER

3

THE RISE OF EGYPT

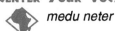
MENES UNITES THE NILE VALLEY

Egypt became a united state with one ruler many years after the first signs of culture appeared along the Nile. Its development began after many years of human activity in the Nile Valley. Starting in the south of the country, the civilization spread throughout the Nile Valley. Finally the north was conquered by the great king Menes, also called Narmer. He was the first pharaoh to govern the entire Nile Valley from the first cataract to the Delta. He built his capital city at Memphis, about 12 miles from present day Cairo.

Menes started the first *dynasty,* or ruling family. After Menes, all pharaohs would pass down the right to rule to their children or other relatives. The first dynasty of Menes is usually dated from around 3100 B.C.E.

THE ROSETTA STONE

Before the early 19th century, the world knew little about ancient Africa because no one could read the ancient Egyptian language. Then, in 1799, the French Army stumbled upon a stone written in the language of ancient Egypt near the town of Rosetta. It would take another 20 years, but the writing on the Rosetta stone would finally be the key to reading the ancient Egyptian language, opening the door to reading other ancient African writings.

The Rosetta stone is a solid black slab about 1 meter (4 feet) high and a little more than half a meter (2 1/2 feet) wide. It had the same message written on it in three different scripts. Two were from the ancient Egyptian, but the other one was from Greek. In 1821, a young Frenchman named Jean Champollion figured out how to translate the message on the Rosetta stone by reading the ancient Greek and then translating the Egyptian. Next, he wrote down the whole Egyptian alphabet. The door to reading the ancient African writings was now open. The secrets of ancient papyruses, temples, and tomb walls could now be understood in all their richness.

▲ The Rosetta stone

No one had been able to read the Rosetta stone at first because the ancient Africans did not speak English, Greek, or Arabic. They spoke an African language which Kemetologists, those who study ancient Egypt, call *medu neter*. The ancient Egyptians also had their own writing system, which was a mix of pictograms,

▲ Hieroglyphs on the wall of a temple in Egypt.

signs, symbols, and syllables. *Pictograms* are pictures that stand for words or letters. The Greeks would call this language *hieroglyphics*. Now that hieroglyphics could be read and understood, the lives of ancient Egyptian royalty as well as the everyday people could be understood in detail.

CENTER YOUR THINKING

1. Name the first person to govern the entire Nile Valley of ancient Egypt.

2. Explain why the first pharaoh was important, and what he passed on to his children and the world.

3. CRITICAL THINKING: Describe the Rosetta stone. How did the Rosetta stone help the world learn about ancient African history and culture?

CHAPTER 4
THE DUAL ROLE OF THE KING

HARMONY AND BALANCE

In the thinking of the ancient Africans, the world was a continuum of good and bad, order and chaos, life and death. All these opposites had to be united in harmony and perfect balance. Disturbing the perfect balance meant that the gods might get angry and cause harm and even destruction.

The king or queen was a dual being to the ancient Africans. The king stood for the ancient African idea of duality, or opposite forces within the same being. The king united and balanced the opposites of the world, creating harmony.

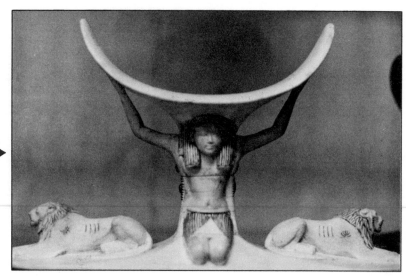

The perfect balance of the pharaoh's role is reflected even in this pharaoh's headrest.

The king ruled all. The king wore two crowns, the red crown and the white crown to represent the two opposite pillars of kingship. As a dual being, the king was both high and low, good and bad, in the same person. The king had to have power and control over the entire world with all its opposite elements.

The idea of omnipresence was part of the ancient African idea of the king. *Omni* means "all." The king was present in all places, all ways, all the time, controlling all the opposing forces in the world and keeping them in harmony and unity. Sometimes in ancient Egyptian writings, the king is called *King of the Two Lands*. This does not mean that the king ruled two different countries. It is a synonym for the paired opposites of the world existing in perfect unity.

THE POWER OF THE PHARAOH

The kings of Egypt were called *pharaohs*. The name *pharaoh* meant "great house" and was used much as we use the term *White House* to stand for the power and authority of the president of the United States. The pharaoh was very powerful and controlled the land and the wealth.

The ancient Egyptians considered the pharaoh to be a god, a divine being. Although many local and lesser gods were also worshiped, the ancient Egyptians considered the pharaoh to be their national deity or god.

Obeying and supporting the pharaoh meant doing good for the well-being of the entire society. To disobey or hurt the pharaoh meant that the entire society and everyone's well-being were

The elaborately decorated stool of ▶ the pharaoh Tutankhamen reflects both the power and the balance or duality of the pharaoh.

hurt. The pharaoh's physical strength and wisdom were connected to all the gods, nature, and the obedience of the people. Again, the perfect harmony and unity that the pharaoh brought to the world of the ancient Africans was extremely important to them in all ways, spiritual, emotional, and physical.

Since the pharaoh was worshiped as god, there were many religious and ceremonial occasions. One very important festival for a king who ruled for 30 years was the Jubilee Festival. During this festival the king had to demonstrate to the priests that he or she was strong enough to conquer a strenuous physical course. The king's stamina was tested on a long obstacle course where the priests had prepared various barriers to be overcome such as small holes, rock piles, and walls. The ancient Africans believed that if their pharaoh could successfully finish the physical tasks, he or she was still strong enough to rule them. They took it as a sign that they should have confidence in the pharaoh.

The pharaoh was responsible for all the building and construction in the country, but he or she could not complete all these jobs alone. Many nobles helped the pharaoh rule the country. They were engineers, merchants, shipbuilders, tax collectors, scribes, and priests, as well as workers. They all did what the pharaoh decided. If canals were dug, minerals were mined, or palaces built, then the pharaoh and many nobles were involved.

CENTER YOUR THINKING

1. What were the kings of Egypt called? Explain the king's role of duality.

2. How might the king's duality have caused problems for the people of ancient Africa? Explain your reasoning.

3. How might the king's role have caused the ancient Egyptians to feel secure and well protected?

CHAPTER 5

KEMET, THE BLACK LAND

VOCABULARY
indigenous   descendant

CENTER YOUR VOCABULARY
 complexion

THE COMPLEXION OF EGYPT

Hundreds of villages dotted the banks of the Nile River. The many different peoples of Egypt were connected from north to south by the great River Nile. Egypt was defined by the course of the Nile River. Egyptian civilization itself was defined by the course of the Nile River. Traders sailed up and down the entire length of the Nile.

The Nile flows from the inside of Africa, from the mountains and hills of the southern highland areas, down into the valleys of the north. Southern Egypt was called Upper Egypt, and Lower

Two Egyptian boys on camels today ▶
evoke memories of ancient Egypt.

Egypt was the north. The Nile flows from the southern highlands of Upper Egypt and empties into the Mediterranean Sea in the north.

The ancient African people affectionately called their land *Kemet,* or the Black Land. Later, the Greeks would give it the name of *Egypt, or Aigyptos,* meaning "the temples of the god Ptah."

Kemet, like *Sudan* and *Ethiopia,* means something like Land of the Blacks or Land of the Africans. Today, if you go to Egypt, the area of ancient Kemet, you will see many African people who look no different from most African Americans.

A term often used to mean "black" in Egypt is *Nubian.* This term is derived from the ancient civilization of Nubia, which was closely related to Egypt both politically and culturally. In fact, the favorite name for African Americans among the Egyptians from Luxor southward is *Nubian Americans.* The term *Nubian* has come to mean those Egyptians who have black skin.

Of course, there is also a large Arab population in Egypt today, with lighter skin tones. Sometimes when people look at

▼ Egyptians today look much like African Americans.

▲ Laurel Darling, an African American from the Cleveland schools, is on the left. Monn Lisa, a Nubian Egyptian, is on the right.

▲ This boy is African American.

Egypt today, they are confused by the many different complexions of the people. However, it is clear in the minds of most Egyptians and scholars that ancient Egyptians looked more like the present-day Nubians than the present-day Arabs. Much like the United States, ancient Egypt attracted many people. The Nile River served as a highway for the meeting of the indigenous

Dr. Molefi Kete Asante, an African ▶ American and the author of this book, and two Egyptians. Can you tell which is Dr. Asante?

Dr. Asante is in the middle.

Africans with people from the outside. The Nubians are the direct descendants of the people who built the massive stone monuments in the Nile Valley. The ancient Egyptians ranged in complexion and build, just as present-day African Americans, African Brazilians, Ethiopians, and Nigerians differ.

The complexions of the skin of the ancient Africans ranged from beautiful chocolates to beautiful vanillas. As we can see from history, the majority of the people of the Black Land were very dark in skin tone.

CENTER YOUR THINKING

1. What did the ancient Africans call their land along the Nile River? Why do you think the Greeks changed the name to *Egypt?*

2. In Egypt today, the people in Upper Egypt (the south) often refer to African Americans as Nubian Americans. Explain what *Nubian American* means to Egyptians today.

3. CRITICAL THINKING: The present population of Egypt is mostly Arab. Write a brief research report on the coming of the Arabs from Arabia to Egypt. Tell the date they arrived and the religion they brought with them to Africa.

CHAPTER 6
EGYPTIAN CULTURE & RELIGION

VOCABULARY

eternal   caste
noble

CENTER YOUR VOCABULARY

 myth

THE MYTHS OF ANCIENT EGYPT

In Upper Egypt, the southern part of the country, there is evidence that the idea of eternal life was highly regarded and was linked to agriculture. The Egyptians were great observers of nature. Because the Nile River overflowed its banks from July to October every year, the people had a fairly good idea about when to try to plant food crops. But, like us, they wanted to understand more about their world. They wanted to understand the mysterious cycles that gave them food and flood, life and death.

The Egyptians developed *myths,* or stories, about gods to explain the mysteries of life. The Egyptians had a rich religious life, with many myths about death and rebirth. Some of these centered around the Nile. The myths were a way for the priests of the various temples to explain the flooding of the Nile River.

To understand the Egyptians, you must understand how important some of their religious myths were to them. The Egyptians were a highly spiritual people. The myths of creation had a special appeal to the majority of them. The Egyptian people were pleased with their beautiful valley which seemed to

SOME ANCIENT EGYPTIAN GODS AND GODDESSES

Horus,
God of the Sky;
also, the Living Ruler

Osiris,
God of the Afterworld;
also of Death, Rebirth,
and Agriculture

Amen,
Sun God;
Great God of the
City of Thebes

Ra,
Sun God;
Great God of the
City of Heliopolis

Ptah,
Sun God;
Great God of the
City of Memphis

Isis,
Mother Goddess,
Protector of the Dead,
wife of Osiris, and
Mother of Horus

Hapi,
God of the Nile

Tehuti,
Ibis-Headed God
of Writing and
Intelligence

them to be a gift from the gods. And they believed that the abundant growth of their vegetables and fruits were explained by their myths of death and rebirth.

THE OSIRIAN MYTH

The myth of the god Osiris explained agriculture as the death and rebirth of the land. Osiris was revered as a god and was associated with water and the rise and fall of the Nile. Every year when the Nile overflowed its banks, the people were reminded of the god Osiris. On the various temples and in the many shrines the people painted pictures of Osiris alongside the various other deities in ancient Africa. The Nile River, called the River Hapi by the Egyptians, gave the people the opportunity to plant their crops in land revitalized by the annual deposit of silt.

THE EGYPTIAN CASTE SYSTEM

The people of ancient Egypt had different jobs, responsibilities, and duties. Career paths and jobs were not decided by choice.

They were decided by the *caste,* or class, of society into which a person was born. The skills of the person were also important.

At the top of the society was the pharaoh, who was untouchable by the common people. The pharaoh was a god and held the keys to the society. But the pharaoh did not make all the decisions.

A ruling caste of priests and nobles efficiently carried out the elaborate tasks and ceremonies in the name of various gods, on behalf of the pharaoh. It was believed that the gods controlled the world, but the people believed that the priests knew how to keep the gods happy. The power and responsibility of the priests were shown in the jobs they chose. Priests could be scribes who wrote all the official documents, doctors, architects, and legal experts. A scribe was an official, usually a priest trained in the use of hieroglyphics, who was entrusted with recording all significant events. A person became a noble by being accorded a high position in the government. Nobles were mayors, provincial rulers, generals, and ministers of the pharaoh.

▼ Egyptian society was based on a caste system. You were born into your caste, or social position and role. The majority of ancient Egyptians were farmers and peasants, at the bottom of the society.

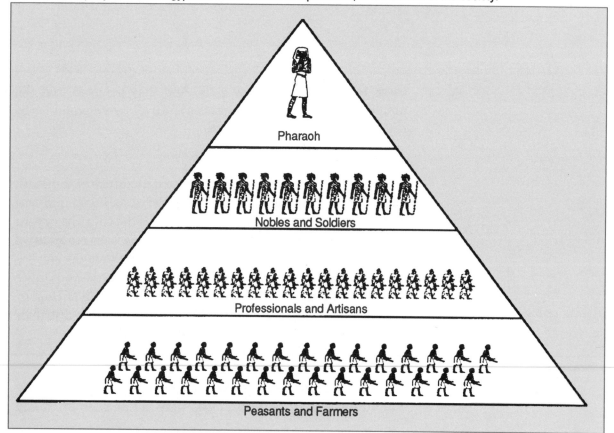

Pharaoh

Nobles and Soldiers

Professionals and Artisans

Peasants and Farmers

Sometimes, craftspersons and soldiers were part of the ruling caste, too, depending on their craft or military duty and how it was valued by society and the pharaoh. Some soldiers, artisans, jewelers, musicians, and architects were seen as part of the ruling caste. The system was flexible to the extent that the pharaoh could change a person's status by bestowing special favor.

For the most part, the laborers and soldiers were part of a middle caste of people with everyday jobs. They were like the middle class in the United States. They served the pharaoh as soldiers or laborers. These were professionals who carried out the day-to-day functions of the society.

The largest group/caste of people in Egypt were farmers, who planted small farms along the banks of the Nile. Most were peasants who barely subsisted on the food they grew. When the floods came and inundated their plots, the farmers were often employed on building projects for the pharaoh.

The farmers did not own their land. The pharaoh, who owned all the land, gave them land to farm. But the gift of land was not free. The pharaoh owned most of the crops grown on the land. Most farmers tried to grow a lot on their land. They had to, or they would not have any food left for themselves and their families. A farmer had to meet a requirement of giving more than half of the crop to the government.

CENTER YOUR THINKING

1. Explain how religious myths may have kept the ancient Egyptians content, peaceful, and happy.

2. Review ways that ancient Egyptians used their knowledge about agriculture to provide for their families.

3. Compare the ancient Egyptian caste system with the economic classes of today's world. List at least one similarity and one difference.

CHAPTER

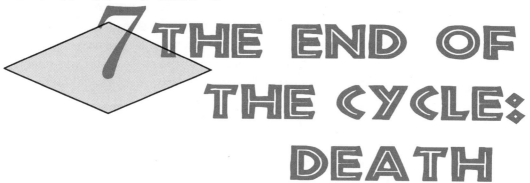

7 THE END OF THE CYCLE: DEATH

LIFE AFTER DEATH

Every culture and religion has beliefs about death and what happens to the body and soul after death, and the Egyptians had specific beliefs about death and the afterlife. They believed that the soul could live forever, but only in the body. Preserving the body, the *ka,* was not just important; it was essential.

The ancient Egyptian mummies in museums today are incredibly well preserved. Some are as old as 5,000 years. To preserve the body, or *ka,* the Egyptians wrapped it in 16 layers of fine linen. These wrapped, preserved bodies are what we call *mummies* today.

In ancient Egypt, life after death was believed to be a continuation of the happy life on earth — but only if the body and tomb were properly preserved and prepared. Egyptian tombs were prepared like rooms in which to live. On the walls were pictures of the daily life of the dead person, who was now a mummy. The dead were buried with things they had used during their lives.

Mummies lasted for thousands of years in the dry Egyptian climate. Many mummies would

An Egyptian mummy, unwrapped, is still well preserved after 3,000 years. ▼

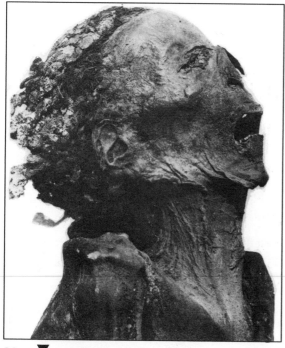

have lasted even longer except for grave robbers. Grave robbers stole the items left in tombs, and they stole and destroyed mummies, too.

The art of mummification was used to prevent deterioration of the corpse. In the beginning, the mummification process was very simple. Organs of the body, such as the heart, liver, and kidneys, were removed and the part of the body cavity where they had been was filled with wads of linen cloth. The corpse was then saturated with a chemical called *natron* and wrapped in linen cloth.

After several hundred years, the Egyptians improved the embalming process to make it even more complete. The brain was removed from the skull by using an iron hook. Various waxes and pastes were applied to the body to preserve it. More than 70 days were needed before all the different tasks of mummification could be completed and the body ready for final burial.

Although the dead cannot talk, much of what we know about ancient life in Egypt comes from the tombs. Paintings on tomb walls of kings, queens, and nobles show that the ancient Africans of this valley grew grains, vegetables, and fruits of all kinds. Although deserts surrounded the Egyptians on both sides of the Nile River Valley, the valley itself was fertile and rich. It permitted many abundant varieties of life to flourish.

CENTER YOUR THINKING

1. How did the ancient Egyptians feel about death and the afterlife?

2. Explain why the Egyptians believed that preserving the *ka* was essential.

3. **CRITICAL THINKING:** How have ancient mummies helped the world to understand the Egyptian concept of eternity? Explain your reasoning.

SUMMARY

 The continent of Africa is incredibly diverse in geography and climate. (p. 9) The earliest organized civilization grew up along the Nile River and lived in civilized peace. (p. 15) However, the ancient Egyptians were a mystery to modern scholars until modern scholars decoded the Rosetta stone and began to understand the ancient language, *medu neter.* (p. 18) We now know that an ancient Egyptian's role in life was determined in large part by caste, or the class of society into which a person was born. (p. 28)

 Thousands of years of ancient African knowledge and scholarship traveled to what was then Persia and on to the Greek civilization when the Greeks studied with African scholars during the second classical season from 525 B.C.E. to 641 C.E. (p. 11)

 Many African Americans look like the ancient Nubians. Egyptians today often call African Americans "Nubian Americans." (p. 24)

 During the ancient classical season from 6000 B.C.E. to 525 B.C.E., important classical African traditions, art forms, religious beliefs, and concepts developed that are part of our culture today. (pp. 10-11)

 During the third classical season from 641 C.E. to 1600 C.E., Africans were feverishly struggling with new beliefs and ideas, including the religion of Islam. (p. 12)

 Ancient Africans believed in the concept of *duality,* or the perfect harmony and balance needed in the world. (p. 20) The ruler was a god, and his or her physical stamina was important or he or she would not be strong enough to balance the opposing forces and keep the world in harmony. (p. 22) The Egyptians also believed that, after death, the soul could only live in the preserved body. (p. 30)

PERSONAL WITNESSING

REFLECTION

Why is it beneficial for you to study African civilization in a class such as this one? For yourself, make a list of reasons why you think it is important for all Americans to study Africa. What else do you want to learn about Africa?

TESTIMONY

Analyze the three seasons of ancient Egyptian history. Tell about them in writing or in another format of your choosing, letting your personal interests in art, sculpture, poetry, and agriculture guide you.

"The names of nearly all our gods came from Egypt into Greece."

— Herodotus

MARVELOUS AFRICA

The ancient African country of Egypt laid the foundation for much of modern civilization. Among its contributions are medicine, the calendar, geometry, and art. No nation in antiquity made as many early contributions to human knowledge as ancient Egypt. Its reputation is established in medicine, mathematics, architecture, religion, and literature.

CENTER YOURSELF

Science is central to the development of the modern world. If you imagine yourself living in classical Africa, you would see new scientific discoveries and achievements all around you. What ancient African discoveries about human life, the earth, the rivers, the sun, birds, and animals would amaze you?

This wonderful statue of Tutankhamen shows advanced artistic style. He is shown realistically from his features to his skin tone and in all the splendor of his time.

CHAPTER 8
EXTRAORDINARY AFRICAN PERSONALITIES

IMHOTEP: THE FATHER OF MEDICINE

Imhotep lived around 2980 B.C.E. and devoted his intellect to the service of one of the earliest Egyptian kings, Zoser. Among the many high-ranking positions Imhotep held as a leading citizen and vizier of ancient Egypt were:

- prime minister
- physician
- priest
- architect

The title of prime minister, called *vizier,* was second in importance to the king. The vizier had the greatest responsibility and power next to the king. Of all the viziers of ancient Egypt, Imhotep was one of the most respected.

Imhotep was also one of the most intelligent viziers. Once Egypt was in desperate trouble because the Nile River had not flooded enough for seven years. The land had suffered through seven years of famine and many people were starving to death. King Zoser called upon the wise Imhotep. When Imhotep came to Zoser, the king asked him, "Why has this calamity befallen our country? What is the birthplace of the Nile?" The king believed that if he could determine the Nile's source, he could alter the flow of the river for the benefit of his people.

Because he could not answer the question immediately, Imhotep asked the king to give him time to think about the question. Then he researched the question in the sacred books.

After a while, he reappeared before King Zoser with his answer in words that had never been spoken to a king before. He revealed to the king the hidden knowledge of the sources of the Nile. It is believed that Imhotep told the king that the origin, or birthplace, of the Nile was in the highlands of Nubia. In fact, this is one source, the Blue Nile, of the Nile. The other source, the White Nile, is in Uganda.

When King Zoser had Imhotep's information, he sent a letter to Meter, the king of Nubia. Zoser asked for Meter's advice on how to increase the flow of water in the Nile so that it would once again flood and enrich the soil. Then the farmers of Egypt would be able to plant and harvest more than enough food to feed everyone.

Meter gave Zoser the idea that he should pay tribute to the god of the source of the Nile, Khnum, to end the famine. Zoser then made a decree, or law, that the Temple of Khnum should be given ivory, ebony, spices, precious stones, and woods. After the king's decree had been carried out, the god Khnum appeared to him in a dream. Khnum promised that the Nile would rise and flood as usual and would never fail again. And it did not, at least not in Imhotep's lifetime.

The ancient Egyptians may have known Imhotep best for ending the famine, but today he is well known as a great architect. He was the chief of the royal building works. His greatest achievement was the building of the famous pyramid at Sakkara, called the Step Pyramid. This was the first pyramid that was used as a king's tomb. It was a transition between the mastaba, the boxlike tombs, and the real pyramids that would be built later around 2800 B.C.E. to 2500 B.C.E. The Step Pyramid is the earliest monument built out of cut stone. It represents the victory of human beings over the use of stone on a grand scale.

▲ The Step Pyramid, built about 2800 B.C.E. by Imhotep for Pharaoh Zoser

Principal Dynasties and Leaders
Dynasty:
1st. **Menes**
2nd. **Peribsen**
3rd. **Zoser**
4th. **Snefru**   **Khufu**   **Khafre**   **Menkaure**
6th. **Teti**   **Pepi I**   **Pepi II**
12th. **Amenemhat I**   **Senusert I**   **Amenemhat II**   **Senusert II**
18th. **Ahmose I**   **Tuthmosis II**   **Hatshepsut**   **Tuthmosis III**   **Amenhotep III**   **Akhenaten**   **Tutankhamen**
19th. **Ramses I**   **Seti I**   **Ramses II**
25th. **Piankhi**   **Shabaka**   **Shabataka**   **Taharka**

In his lifetime, Imhotep was worshiped as a god because of his advances in medicine. He was the first person to make a catalog of human illnesses and to propose treatments for many of them. Indeed, he laid the foundations for the study and practice of medicine. He was later honored by the Greeks, who integrated him into their concept of medicine and worshiped him as a god of medicine, by giving him the Greek name, Asclepios.

However, Imhotep was not the only physician in ancient Africa. There were many other physicians in ancient Egypt. Some of them wrote important books describing illnesses and how to cure them. One of these early books tells how surgery was performed on people with cracked skulls and broken spines! So much of what we know and do to treat diseases was passed down from these ancient Africans, Imhotep and others.

Imhotep is also credited with the building of temples and the development of rituals for worship. So important were the achievements of Imhotep that he was thought of as both man and deity.

The First Woman to Be Pharaoh: Hatshepsut, or Ma'at Ka Re

As ancient Africa's chief classical culture, Egypt was not ruled only by men. The first woman to rule as pharaoh in her own name and by her own power was the 18th dynasty queen, Hatshepsut. When she became pharaoh she took the royal name, Ma'at Ka Re.

Three other women ruled as queens, but only because their husbands had been pharaohs. Only Hatshepsut came to the throne without following her husband. She ruled as a regent, or caretaker, for the boy king, Tuthmosis III, for about three years, but soon took over and ruled in her own name as pharaoh.

Hatshepsut took the title of pharaoh just as the male pharaohs before her had done. She even sometimes wore the false beard, a symbol of authority, just as male pharaohs did. She did not use the title queen, but, instead, called herself king. Neither did she let anyone else use the title of queen in her presence. She gave herself equality with her male predecessors.

Hatshepsut is remembered as one of ancient Egypt's most distinguished leaders. She built beautiful temples and tombs. She raised obelisk after obelisk and stela after stela. These obelisks and stelae bore her name and gave praise to the gods.

▲ The Temple at Karnak

At the Temple of Amen at Karnak, Hatshepsut had monumental statues built in her honor. Obelisks carved out of granite from Aswan were placed in the courtyard of the famous temples at Karnak. All of these public buildings and statuary were evidence of her majesty. Only one of her obelisks is still in its original temple area in Egypt today. Others can be found in New York, Rome, London, Paris, and Istanbul.

The greatest adventure of Hatshepsut's reign was her expedition to Punt (modern day Somalia). This was one of the most talked about adventures in ancient African history. She sent a large group of explorers and traders to the east coast of Africa to interact with the people and trade with them. When the expedition returned to the capital city, Thebes, it brought all kinds of riches, ivory, gold, giraffes, leopards, and special fruits. Hatshepsut's reputation as a great ruler became even more respected.

Hatshepsut had Senmut, an architect and close friend, design and build for her a major temple. She wanted it to be her tomb. The temple built for Hatshepsut is one of the greatest temples built in Egypt. Named for her, it stands in the Valley of the Queens near the modern city of Luxor.

▲ The Temple of Pharaoh Hatshepsut ▶

1. Why was Imhotep highly respected in ancient Egypt and, later, in ancient Greece?

2. How have Imhotep's contributions to the sciences been useful to us?

3. CRITICAL THINKING: Hatshepsut was the first woman pharaoh. List some problems she might have confronted as the first woman pharaoh. What do you think the men thought about her? How did she show her ability and majesty?

9 EARLY AFRICAN SCIENCE & ART

VOCABULARY

geometry   papyrus
colonnade   inscription

CENTER YOUR VOCABULARY

calendar
pylon

MATHEMATICS IN CLASSICAL EGYPT

If, as some have said, mathematics is the single attribute of the human mind which shows how advanced a civilization is, then the Egyptians of Africa who lived several thousand years before Christ had a highly advanced civilization.

We know of two books about mathematics written by the early Africans in Egypt. One is called the *Moscow Papyrus*. The other is called the *Rhind Papyrus*. Both books of mathematical problems existed more than 2,000 years before the civilizations of Greece or Rome.

▼The Temple of Ramses II at Abu Simbel

An advanced ability to measure and to use measurements to create buildings and monuments was certainly a part of ancient African knowledge. The people who constructed the great temples at Memphis, Abydos, Abu Simbel, and Thebes knew a great deal about how to measure things. Using mathematics to determine the right measurements and build huge temples that would last thousands of years was a highly developed skill in classical Africa.

The ancient Africans developed the branch of mathematics known today as *geometry*, meaning "earth measuring." It was originally

▲ The Temple at Thebes could not have been built without an expert knowledge of geometry.

needed to map the boundaries of land around the Nile. If you had land on the banks of the Nile, how else could you know exactly where your farm ended and another farmer's land began? When the Nile flooded each year, your markers might well be destroyed, especially if they were sticks or stones in the ground. After the mighty Nile overflowed its banks, you and your neighbors might have a bitter argument over land!

To avoid arguments, the Egyptians used geometry to measure the land and settle the score over boundaries. They also used geometry to measure the squares, triangles, circles, and cubes used in building pyramids. All of the monuments were built with a mathematical precision that showed the Egyptians to be masters of mathematics.

ASTRONOMY

The ancient Egyptians knew a great deal about the stars and the science of astronomy. We also know that they studied the moon. They were expert record keepers. They kept records for centuries to compare and understand the movements and characteristics of the stars. Using these records, they developed the calendar we use today.

The ancient Egyptians also learned enough to be able to build one pyramid so that its sides were exactly in line with certain stars and planets! The Temple of Ramses II at Abu Simbel was built so that the sun would shine on Ramses II's statue twice each year. It happened every year on his birthday and on the day he had become king. And, even more amazing, Ramses II's statue is inside the temple!

Their knowledge of astronomy and observations of the skies led the ancient Africans to understand that the calendar needed to be 365 1/4 days. We still use this calendar today. It is based on the number of days needed for the Earth to go around the sun one time.

While some of our months today have 31 days, and February has 28 or 29 days, all the months in the Egyptian calendar had 30 days. Five extra holidays followed the last month each year. One of the most important uses of the ancient Egyptian calendar was to tell them exactly when the Nile would rise and flood its banks.

Papyrus

The ancient Africans of Egypt gave the world its first paper, called *papyrus*. The English word *paper* comes from the ancient word *papyrus*. Papyrus is made from the papyrus plant that grows in Africa along the Nile River. It can be dried and used to write on. When the ancient Egyptians did this, they created the first lightweight writing material in history. Ancient Egyptian papyruses have been found with mathematics problems and blueprints for architectural wonders on them.

Architecture

▲ The Great Sphinx

▼ A newly found sphinx, Cairo

The pyramids, the Great Sphinx, and the enormous Temple of Karnak are the most famous and best known examples of all the architectural constructions of the ancient Egyptians.

Eighty pyramids were built in ancient Egypt. Of all these pyramids, the most impressive is the Great Pyramid of Khufu. Khufu was the king whom the Greeks later called Cheops. Today, the Great Pyramid of Khufu is also called the Cheops Pyramid. It was built around 2644 B.C.E. It is one of the wonders of the world.

Two other pyramids, Khafre's and Menkaure's, are also considered to be wonders of the world. The Pyramid of Snefru is the third tallest pyramid, coming before Menkaure's. Its sides have bulges in them and it is called the Crooked Pyramid.

Height & location of the Great Pyramids		
Khufu	146.0 meters	Giza
Khafre	143.5 meters	Giza
Snefru	105.0 meters	Dahshur
Menkaure	65.6 meters	Giza
Zoser	63.0 meters	Sakkara

The Great Sphinx, located close to the Great Khufu Pyramid on the plains of Giza, is still one of the unsolved puzzles in history. It is believed that this structure of a lion with a man's head is more than 15,000 years old. Its purpose and why it was built remain a mystery.

The Temple of Karnak was dedicated to Amen, the god of the city of Thebes, or Luxor today. It is an awesome, fascinating spectacle of courtyards, colonnades, obelisks, and pylons. The temple was not just the biggest building in Africa; it was the biggest building project in the ancient world.

Approaching the temple one sees on either side of the huge gate giant walls of stone, called *pylons,* more than 50 feet high. In ancient times these pylons were decorated with paintings, flags, and banners.

Inside the temple are hundreds of massive columns in rows arranged to show the majesty of the god Amen. Such colonnades are found throughout the temple site.

Amen was the great god of the city of Thebes (Luxor, Egypt, today). The Temple to Amen at Karnak is approached down an avenue of one hundred or more ram-headed sphinxes. The different areas of the building are separated by six massive walled gateways. The huge size of the temple is one of the great achievements of Egyptian classical architecture. Earlier sacred sites in this area of Africa had been small shrines made of reeds, or plants. At these ancient shrines, the priest made offerings to local gods. With the construction of stone temples such as the one at Karnak, Egyptian classical architecture reached new heights in architectural skill. The Egyptians now built avenues lined with sphinxes. These

▲ The Temple to Amen at Karnak ▶

majestic and mysterious lions with the heads of human, rams or hawks lined connecting walkways between temples. Sometimes they stood guard at the entrances to great ancient sites.

The Great Sphinx at Giza is one of the most visited monuments in the world. Its age is unknown, though some suspect it might be close to 15,000 years old.

People still come from all over the world to see the Pyramids, the Temple of Hatshepsut, the tombs of Ramses and Meriruka, the Temples at Karnak and Luxor, and the giant temple statues at Abu Simbel. They are surprised at the quality of the ancient construction. They ask what everyone asks: How did the Africans cut these large stones, some of them weighing 15 tons, and place them on top of each other? We may never solve the ancient mysteries. We still call the Great Pyramid of Khufu one of the Seven Wonders of the Ancient World. It is the only one of the wonders that still stands today.

Sculpture and Painting

From what we have found still in existence today, it seems that no ancient civilization was as rich in painting and sculpture as classical Egypt. The whole country seemed to be engaged in either painting the walls of temples and tombs or carving massive statues of human beings and animals, particularly those animals that represented the gods. Just a few of the many animals that stood for gods were rams, cows, cats, crocodiles, and lions.

The paintings on the walls of the ancient buildings are the main way in which we have learned how the ancient Egyptians lived. There were no television shows or films then, but the ancient paintings give us a picture of Egypt as seen through ancient Egyptian eyes.

For instance, from these ancient paintings, we know how the Egyptians built their ships, cut stone, harvested wheat, buried their dead, hunted for birds, fought their enemies, and related to the opposite sex.

Some of the sculptures are so lifelike that when I saw them in the Cairo and Luxor museums, I felt

▲ A drawing of the god, Hathor

▼ Sculpture of a priest

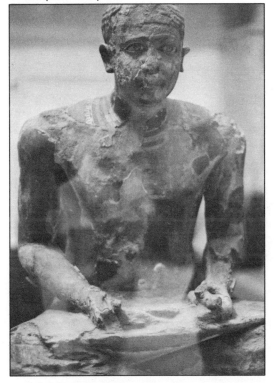

▲ A drawing of the god Tehuti, the Egyptian god of literature

they were about to speak to me. The statue of Amenhotep, Son of Hapu, in the Luxor Museum, is so vibrant and real that it beckons you to talk with it. And I had the same feeling when I saw the hundreds of lifelike statues in the huge Cairo Museum.

Once you have seen the paintings and sculptures of ancient Africa, you know that they will never be forgotten. And you will also realize that many of our modern painting and sculpture techniques have come from them, especially from Egypt and Nubia. Our African link with the past has given us great inspiration, inspiration that is alive today.

LITERATURE

The classical Egyptians believed that the god of literature was Tehuti (or Thoth). They used the figure of an ibis, a bird, to represent him. Sometimes he is shown holding a pen. The ancient Egyptians believed that Tehuti taught human beings to write and showed them what to write. From the earliest times of the great pyramids and temples, writing existed in Egypt. The first writings we know about are inscriptions on monuments, labels, records of the number of cows someone owned, and writing about the achievements of the king. The first writing usually studied in the history of the world is Egyptian. The early Africans of the Nile Valley wrote on coffins, temples, tombs, and papyrus.

The Egyptian *Book of the Dead* is a collection of writings about life and death. It reminds me of the Bible in many ways. One good example that sounds similar to the Bible is the words of the Negative Confessions or, as they are called, the 42 Principles of Ma'at. Some of them are translated below:

> *"I have not done evil."*
> *"I have not robbed with violence."*
> *"I have not stolen."*
> *"I have not made any to suffer pain."*
> *"I have done no murder nor bid anyone to slay on my behalf."*
> *"I have not cheated anyone."*
> *"I have not spoken lies."*
> *"I have not robbed God."*
> *"I have not caused the shedding of tears."*
> *"I have not stopped my ears against the words of right and truth."*

1. What are the names of the two mathematics books written by ancient Africans in Egypt? How long before the civilizations of Greece or Rome did they exist?

2. It is said that ancient Africans contributed the calendar to our civilization. What is a calendar? Why is a calendar important? What happens if you do not have a calendar?

3. CRITICAL THINKING: Explain some of the special skills that were needed for the ancient Africans to be architects, surveyors, and astronomers. What problems might have occurred in building if they had not invented the science of geometry? How did the ancient Africans leave us important legacies in literature, architecture, art, and science?

CHAPTER 10 EGYPTIAN RELIGION

VOCABULARY

god	procession
narrative	controversy

CENTER YOUR VOCABULARY

theology
creation

THE HOME OF NEARLY ALL THE GODS

Egypt, according to a Greek historian named Herodotus, is the home of the name of nearly all the gods. While it may be overstated to say that Egypt was the home of all the gods, Egypt certainly had many gods. The following are only a few.

> *Atum,* the Almighty
>
> *Ptah,* the Almighty
>
> *Ra,* the Almighty
>
> *Amen,* the Hidden
>
> *Heru,* protection
>
> *Auset,* motherhood, love
>
> *Mut,* war
>
> *Montu,* war
>
> *Khnum,* the Creator
>
> *Hathor,* fertility
>
> *Anubis,* judgment
>
> *Hu,* the Word
>
> *Ausar,* agriculture
>
> *Ma'at,* balance, justice
>
> *Tehuti,* literature, knowledge

There were hundreds more gods than listed here. Each god had a special function. For example, Hu was responsible for good speech and good writing. Ausar was responsible for agriculture and resurrection. Hathor was responsible for happiness and fertility.

Each god was represented by a particular animal or human image. Sobek, for instance, was represented by a crocodile. Anubis was a hyena. Tehuti was a bird called an ibis. Hathor was a cow.

THE SUPREME GODS OF EGYPT

Atum, Ra, Ptah, and Amen were the supreme gods in ancient Egypt. Atum and Ra were worshipped at the city of Heliopolis. Ptah was worshiped at Memphis. Amen was worshiped at Thebes.

Whenever any one god was worshiped by all the people of Egypt, that god was supreme and the only god for a time. Imagine what it must have meant to the people of Egypt to see the procession of a supreme god moving from the river Nile to the great temple. Dressed in the sacred robes of their office, the priests would sing praises to the god as they walked, carrying ceremonial flails and staffs in their hands.

Egypt, like other later African countries, was a land of many gods. There was always a supreme god in ancient Egypt, but other gods were important to the people. These gods were responsible both for many important qualities and for everyday skills and needs. Ma'at was the god of justice. Tehuti was the god of writing. Imhotep was the god of medicine.

The chief gods were always gods of the sun: Atum, Ra, Ptah, and Amen. Each one was the special god of a city and had his own priests and priesthood. At one time, 3,000 priests were connected with the temple to Amen. It was the responsibility of the priests to interpret the theology, or the religious philosophy and beliefs, of the gods.

Each of the four supreme gods had a specific theology. The four theologies were similar, but not exactly alike. Each was different, for example, in how they explained the creation of the world.

THE DIFFERENT NARRATIVES OF CREATION

The two major narratives of creation in the classical world are called the Heliopolis version and the Memphis version. Each story was argued about from time to time. In the city of Heliopolis, Atum was supreme, the great god. In Memphis, however, the priests taught that Ptah was the only god. Both theologies were based on their creation stories.

The basic story line in both narratives starts out the same. God (of course, two different gods) created all the other gods and all humans, plants, and animals. But how each god created the world is different in each narrative. According to the Heliopolis creation story, the supreme god created the other gods in a very human way — by having children as humans do. According to the Memphis creation story, however, the supreme god created the world by his thoughts and words. Another difference between the two creation-stories part of the narrative that is different is the identity of the supreme god. In Heliopolis, God was Atum; in Memphis, God was Ptah.

THE ATEN CONTROVERSY

The power of the priests of Amen grew very great during the 18th dynasty, or about 1,500 years before the birth of Christ. At this time, a young king named Amenhotep IV

▲ A statue of Akhenaten

became the great pharaoh. He was deeply disturbed that the priests of Amen had so much power that they could tell him what to do. They asked him for special gifts for the temples, food, clothing allowances, money for sacrifices, and money for repairing the holy sites.

The priests of Amen had become so wealthy and powerful that the head priests, led by two high priests, Suti and Her, controlled hundreds of additional priests. These priests helped with the functions of the religion, much like preachers in churches today. Thousands of people had to be taken care of each day and on special high holy days. To do this, the priests needed money for their 83 ships, 46 worksites where they quarried special stones and minerals, 450,000 animals they used to sacrifice, and the many acres of farmland they had to run, on which crops were raised to feed the priests and other people who served the great temples!

The king refused to grant the priests anything they wanted. In fact, he went so far as to challenge their authority to be priests and to worship the god Amen. They had offended him with their statements about how great the god Amen was and how Amen had made him pharaoh. They probably pointed out to him that his very name, *Amenhotep,* meant "one who satisfies Amen."

The king did not believe in Amen. He believed in Aten. And he was certainly not pleased with the priests of Amen. So he had a thought, a truly revolutionary thought at the time.

Amenhotep decided that, since he was king, he would make Aten, the sun disk that you see in the sky, the one supreme god to be worshiped in Egypt. He then became to preach his own religious theology. He said that there was but one god and his name was Aten.

Predictably, the priests at the temple of Amen were very angry. They considered Aten a very minor almost insignificant god, or deity. This new theology seemed sacrilegious to them. They already had a respected major god for the sun, the god Ra. They did not see how the outline of the sun, the disk of the sun, could be so important.

Nevertheless, the king Amenhotep pushed forward with his ideas. He got some priests together and proclaimed that they were the priests of Aten. He built a small temple between

▲ Avenue of the Sphinxes

the two great temples of Thebes, right on the Avenue of the Sphinxes. The priests of Amen had to walk past the new temple each time they took the god Amen to see the female god Mut.

The young king was either very bold or very crazy. He moved his capital city far away from Thebes. Remember that Thebes may have been the oldest known city in the ancient world at the time. It was the greatest city in Egypt. It had more important sites and people, temples, universities, doctors, sesh (or scribes), artists, and artisans than any other place in the world at that time. But the young king decided to move the capital, anyway, and so he did.

Amenhotep thought that by moving the capital, he would be respected more by the people. He would have his own capital city and a group of priests who upheld his idea that Aten was the only god. Some people have even said he was the first to come up with the idea of one supreme god. This is not true, but he was the first to argue so boldly for the idea. He was the most prominent official in the ancient world to promote the idea of one god.

Amenhotep moved his capital to a place now called Tell el-Marna. He named his new capital after the god Aten. Of course, he would first have to rename himself after Aten. So he did. He no longer called himself Amenhotep to praise the god Amen. He now called himself Akhenaten to praise the name of Aten. Then he named his new capital city Akhetaten.

▲ Akhenaten

But Aten was not to last long as the god of Egypt. After 15 years, the revolt of Akhenaten against the god Amen came to an end. The king was overthrown and probably killed. A new king took the throne. He moved the capital back to the ancient city of Thebes. The priests of Thebes received the new royal family. They made sacrifices of food and animals to the god Amen for the return to their theology.

Akhenaten had tried a bold idea. His poetry in praise of Aten and his devotion to an new idea would inspire many generations of Africans and other people of the world. Some would erroneously proclaim him the "father of monotheism."

UNIT REVIEW

◆ SUMMARY

 The advancements in classical Africa that laid the foundations for modern science, mathematics, and art include advances in medicine by ancient African physicians (p. 36), and the development of geometry. (pp. 39-40)

 Classical Africa rulers, or pharaohs, were both men and women. Hatshepsut is one of the most fondly remembered women to rule as pharaoh. (pp. 36-37)

 Most of the gods that appear in classical Greek and Roman religions originated in Egypt. Many of the gods who appear in classical mythology and literature appear first in different Egyptian religions. (p. 46)

 The quest for knowledge along with a feeling of a spiritual link with nature and a need to understand nature are human needs that date back to classical Africa with Zoser's quest to find the birthplace of the Nile River. (p. 35)

 The painting and sculpture of ancient Africa still seem so realistic and alive that our link to the past makes classical Africa seem only a year away. The change to a realistic style, a style that captures the personality as well as the physical features of people, a style that captures feelings and emotions as well as actions, clearly developed in ancient African culture. (p. 44)

PERSONAL WITNESSING

REFLECTION

Think about how an ancient Egyptian might have developed a story explaining the creation of the world. List some important things that would need to be included. Create your own creation story.

TESTIMONY

Think about the word *civilization.* Decide what you think it means to have a civilization. Share with your colleagues the ideas you have for civilizing your own city. What should be done to improve the civilization in big cities? in suburban areas? in the countryside?

"Nubia is the mother of Egypt."
— **John Jackson**

NUBIA: ANCIENT AND SUPREME

Nubia has been compared to Egypt in Africa and, at times, has controlled Egypt from its own capital cities.

CENTER YOURSELF

Imagine a beautiful Nubian queen walking along the Nile as she talks with members of her royal court. What issues would she discuss with her court officials? What topics would you have discussed if you had been queen or king of Nubia?

Taharka was the most distinguished African pharaoh in the Nubian period, but there were many great Nubian leaders, both men and women.

CHAPTER 11
HISTORICAL PERIODS OF NUBIA

VOCABULARY

ostrakon   convert

CENTER YOUR VOCABULARY

prehistoric

PREHISTORIC NUBIA

Nubia was a very old civilization. Nubian culture appeared as early as 6,000 years before the Common Era. Although this early period is called prehistoric, it is not reasonable to assume that cave dwellers who could barely communicate with each other were the prehistoric inhabitants. We should remind ourselves that *prehistoric* simply means there is no written information about the culture during that period. It does not mean that there was no culture.

For prehistoric Nubia, we have many ways to learn about the culture. There are Nubian paintings on rocks, pottery, and the symbols on ostrakons, for example. An *ostrakon* is a piece of broken pottery with either designs or writing on the outside.

Archaeologists and researchers who look for this evidence have been able to determine the age of the Nubian culture from the remains of clay pots, vases, and other objects.

From the ancient fragments of Nubian prehistory, we learn that Nubian culture was very creative. The people developed religious and political concepts that were the basis for later developments in the Nile Valley. For example, the ostrakons show elements of writing that formed the core of a script, or writing style, seen in the later cultures of Egypt and Nubia.

Abu Simbel
Faras
Halfa
Semna   Saras
Diago
Karma
Dongola   Argo
Nile River
Nuri
Old Dongloa   Karima
Meroe
KUSH
Meroe
Shendi
Kabushi
Sabaluka Gorge   Musawwara
Nagaa
Soba

△ Pyramids   O Temples   • Towns

▲ Ancient Nubia

THE EARLY HISTORIC PERIOD IN NUBIA, 3100-2800 B.C.E.

This period in Nubia starts with 3100 B.C.E. simply because that is the date when writing first appeared in Egypt, and that is the date when Nubia is first written about. Nubia probably existed long before this period as a well-developed civilization, judging from the physical evidence we have in pottery, tools, cave paintings, and others artifacts. From these artifacts, we know that Nubian culture existed as early as 6000 B.C.E.

Ta-Seti was the name given to Nubia in ancient Egyptian records. *Ta-Seti* means "Land of the Bow." The Nubian people were great fighters. They had mastered the bow and arrow so well that they fought and conquered smaller kingdoms in the Nile Valley. Through their military power, the Nubians consolidated a group of smaller kingdoms into a single empire in the Nile Valley.

▲ A drawing of the royal pyramids of Nubia

The tombs of the Nubian kings during this period tell a story of power and wealth. They contained great amounts of precious stones, gold, jewelry, beautiful pottery, and luxury items. They were elaborate enough to rival those found in Egypt from the same time period.

We learn from the Egyptian records that Nubia and Egypt interacted as equals during this period. Some scholars suggest that various ideas (monarchy, divine kingship) and creative objects (boats, teapots) were really the creations of Nubians, not Egyptians.

THE RISE OF THE KUSH AND MEROE NUBIAN KINGDOMS, 2000-1500 B.C.E.

The rise of Kush and Meroe was a period of intense trade and contact with Egypt. Trading groups from Nubia (that is, from Kush and Meroe) went to Egypt frequently. The two cultures interacted all along the Nile. In fact, one of the Egyptian kings, Senusert I, was terrified that the kings of Nubia would completely swallow up his kingdom. He began to build a series of fortresses just to watch the activities and movements of the Nubians.

Nubians farmed along the river banks of the Nile. They built new villages and temples. The Nubian kings were buried in large mounds as big as a football field. Nubian kings were not wrapped as mummies as the Egyptians did. Instead, the king's body was placed on a bed of gold and surrounded by valuables made of ivory and gold.

The name of the Nubian kingdom during this period was Kush. This was one of two great Nubian kingdoms that was started during this period. The other great kingdom was Meroe. In years to come, however, these great Nubian kingdoms would be overshadowed by the magnificent ancient kingdom of Axum.

▲ Farming in classical Nubia was much like farming is in Nubia today.

▼ A Nubian village today

The United Period in Nubia, 1,550-750 B.C.E.

The Egyptians fought a 50-year war against the Nubian kingdom of Kush. At the end, the Nubians were defeated and the Egyptians were in control. One of the highest-ranking officials in the Egyptian government was called the King's Son of Kush. He was responsible for governing Nubia for the Egyptians. For hundreds of years, Nubians and Egyptians saw themselves as belonging to the same kingdom.

Nubian and Egyptian cultures mingled, interacting with equality. The gods of Nubia became gods in Egypt and vice versa. Fashions from Nubia and Egypt were interchangeable. In the picture of the earliest ethnology known found in the tomb of Ramses III, the Egyptian and Nubian wear similar dress while the Libyan and Persian are given other styles of dress.

The Tomb of Ramses III, 12th ▶ century B.C.E., has an ethnology of ancient races painted on its walls. The people are, left to right, Egyptian, Libyan, Nubian, and Persian. Would you have guessed this from skin color and features?

▼ The first great capital of Nubia was Napata in Kush.

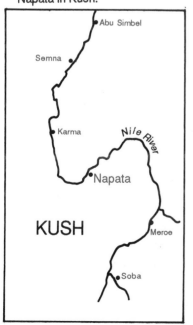

The Napatan Period in Kush (Napata), 750-270 B.C.E.

The first great capital in Nubia was the Kushite city of Napata. Located on the Nile in the country that is now Sudan, this city was very important in the early days of the kingdom as an administrative and commercial center. From here, the kings and queens ruled, and from here, the traders and artisans established the power of Kush.

During this period, Egypt grew weak and the kings from the North could no longer keep Nubia and Egypt united as one kingdom. A powerful king by the name of Piankhi began to build a power base in Napata, the capital city of Nubia. In

724 B.C.E., Piankhi led a mighty army from Kush in the south. The Nubian army defeated the Egyptians.

Piankhi's name meant "the mighty living one," and, during this period, he truly was. After he had seen all of Egypt and conquered all that he saw, he declared himself to be the pharaoh of both Nubia and Egypt.

There is no evidence that Piankhi or, for that matter, the Nubian kings who came later, such as Shabaka, Shabataka, and Taharka, believed that the Egyptians were any better than they were or had more impressive temples. In fact, during this period, many Egyptian temples that had fallen into ruin were rebuilt and remodeled by the ruling Napata dynasty. And, of course, new temples and new tombs were built.

Ruling from their twin capitals of Thebes and Napata, the Nubian pharaohs of Kush built new monuments, new tombs, and new obelisks. There was a neo-Nubian (which means, literally, "new Nubian") revival in Egypt. New Nubian literature was written, also.

The Nubian kingdom of Kush, combining Egypt with Nubia, once again reigned supreme in the Nile Valley. But trouble was on the way. Sitting in their palaces deep in the interior of Africa, the Nubian pharaohs of the 25th dynasty could not keep watch on their northern and eastern borders.

Just as the Nubians were becoming comfortable in their roles as pharaohs of a combined Nubia and Egypt, trouble struck. The Assyrians, from the area that is Iraq today, invaded Egypt in 660 B.C.E. They defeated the combined armies of Nubia and Egypt.

The Assyrians forced many Egyptians to move to Nubia. They made many Nubian officials withdraw from Napata even farther south. These Nubian officials set up a new capital, the city of Meroe. After this period of Assyrian rule, the Nile Valley would never be the same. The Assyrians had shown that the valley could be invaded successfully and controlled. The Persians would eventually conquer the valley in 525 B.C.E. and the Greeks in 333 B.C.E. Although Egypt would turn out to be more vulnerable than Nubia, the handwriting was also on the wall for the great Nubian kingdom of Kush. Kush would last for several hundred more years, but it was now open to danger.

▲ Drawing of a Nubian tomb

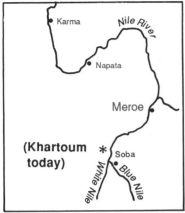

▲ The kingdom of Meroe

THE MEROITIC PERIOD IN NUBIA, 270 B.C.E.-600 C.E.

The Meroe kingdom was known far and wide. In fact, the famous Meroitic script, which many scholars believe holds more information about ancient Africa, is from this region. The Nubian capital at Meroe even held power over regions far south of present day Khartoum.

Having inherited the great ancient traditions of the Nubian people, the Meroitic kingdom upheld the Nubian tradition of conquering those around them. They made annual raids on surrounding kingdoms, conquering them and solidifying their own power.

Traders from Meroe traveled down the Nile, trading with people in the Mediterranean area. They traveled up the Atbara, White Nile, and Blue Nile rivers, trading with their neighbors in the central African region.

THE MEROITIC KINGS OF NUBIA
▼

270 B.C.E.	0		300 C.E.
Arkamani-qp 270-260 B.C.E.	Amanishakheto 10 B.C.E.-0	Natakamani 0-20 C.E.	Yesbokheamani 283-300 C.E.

THE CHRISTIAN KINGDOMS OF NUBIA, 600 - 1000 C.E.

Nubian power declined during the period of the Christian kingdoms. Invaders from Byzantium (Turkey and Greece today) and Egypt brought their Christian religion with them when they came into Nubia. The conquerors converted many to Christianity. Ruins of Nubian Christian churches may be found even today throughout modern Sudan indicating that Nubia had become a vital link in the spread of Christianity.

In fact, Christianity's early roots were in three African nations, Egypt, Nubia (Sudan today), and Ethiopia. For the first time in Africa, Christianity became the strongest religion.

Islam entered Africa in 639-641 C.E. with the conquest of Egypt. It would not be until the 15th century that the religion would defeat the Christian strongholds of Nubia. Combining the might of the Ottoman Turks and the Arabs, the Islamic forces destroyed many churches and scattered the Christians of Nubia by the beginning of the 16th century.

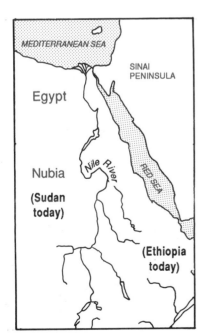

▲ The roots of Christianity were in Egypt, Nubia, and Ethiopia.

The Arabic Conquest (Islam), 1500 C.E. - Present

When the religion of Islam became the leading religion in the 1500s, it finished off many ancient religious customs and influences that had survived Christianity. And once Islam took root, the fate of the Nubian Christians who had fought with the Christian European crusaders to save Jerusalem from Islam was sealed. The Nubian Christians were punished harshly.

The triumphant history and traditions of this ancient African culture and civilization were wiped out during this modern period in history. Much of what was the glorious kingdom of Nubia disappeared in the sands of the desert.

Today, the area once occupied by the ancient African kingdom of Nubia is controlled by the modern country of Sudan. Although Sudan has tried to protect the ancient monuments, the environment and pollution have ruined most of them. Sudan lacks enough money to preserve the ancient monuments properly. Perhaps one day soon, the glory that was ancient Nubia will once again be familiar to the world.

Center Your Thinking

1. Why is the earliest period of Nubian culture known as "prehistoric"? What artifacts helped archaeologists understand prehistoric Nubian culture? What was learned about prehistoric Nubia from these artifacts?

2. If Senusert I and other Egyptians had not been concerned about the mighty Nubian presence just south of them, what might have happened to Egypt? Explain.

3. CRITICAL THINKING: Explain Piankhi's role in helping Nubia and Egypt reign supreme as one kingdom in the Nile Valley, and also explain what happened to the United kingdom of Kush and Meroe. How did the Nile Valley change after the Assyrian conquest?

CHAPTER 12
THE PHYSICAL GEOGRAPHY OF NUBIA

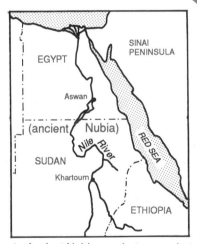

▲ Ancient Nubia was between what is today Aswan and Khartoum.

ANCIENT NUBIA

To find the location of ancient Nubia, you must find the cities of Aswan in Egypt and Khartoum in Sudan today. These are the northern and southern borders of the ancient kingdom of Nubia. The land that was ancient Nubia has not changed much from the way it was. However, the modern day descendants of the ancient Nubian peoples live in the south of Egypt and in the north of the Sudan.

NUBIA AND THE NILE RIVER

Nubia was a child of the Nile River, much like Egypt, or Kemet, in the north. Without the Nile's lifegiving waters, the people of ancient Nubia would have died. Although they were hardy people who hunted in the desert, most of their food came from the Nile. Fish and waterfowl were plentiful.

Like the Egyptians, the Nubians depended upon the annual rainfall in the mountains of what is today Uganda and Ethiopia. These heavy rains made the rich silt, or fertile soil, wash into the Nile. Then the Nile overflowed and gave life to the farmers with the rich land. In the silt deposited on the riverbanks of the Nile, the people grew many different fruits and vegetables during the year, such as oranges and bananas.

▲ Just beyond the lush Nile Valley, the desert takes over immediately.

However, the Nile Valley and the other river valleys are only a small part of Nubia. Desert makes up nearly 95 percent of the land in Nubia. Although the narrow band of land along the Nile is some of the most fertile land anywhere, the land beyond the river is some of the driest on earth. Desert sands and granite rocks often extend right to the edge of the river. There are areas where nothing seems to grow and the land is so dry that it is extremely difficult for humans to live. In upper Nubia, the desert blooms when a little rain falls. The ingenuity of the ancient Nubian people is impressive. They had to use all their creativity simply to survive.

THE BELLY OF ROCKS

Among the features of the Nubian landscape between Aswan and Khartoum are the six major cataracts, areas where rocks jut out of the river and create hazardous waterfalls. People have always traveled up and down the Nile. But they have had to take their boats out of the water and carry them around the cataracts. Often it was easier to travel by land than on the river in the area of the cataracts.

In ancient times, the 60-mile area of rocks between the second and third cataracts was called the *Belly of Rocks.* Many wars took place here. Trapped on the land routes on either side of the river, many soldiers from both Nubian and Egyptian armies died through the years.

Cataracts are beautiful, but they block navigation on the Nile in a most unusual way. Consider thousands of rocks suddenly appearing in the middle of a river. Ships could not pass.

Even worse, cataracts made communication between villages difficult or impossible. Not to be stopped, however, the ingenious Nubians set up a series of villages alongside the cataracts. The villages acted as fortresses, protecting the Nubians from a surprise attack coming from the river.

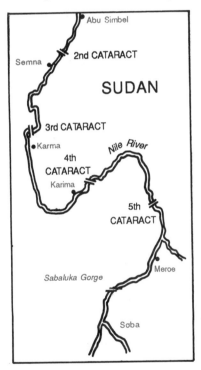

▲ The cataracts of the Nile make navigation hazardous.

Nubia: The Gateway of History

Probably no other nation, with the possible exception of Turkey, has so often been called the gateway to some other place. Turkey, we are often told, is the gateway to Asia or the gateway to Europe, depending on one's orientation. Nubia is often called the gateway to Africa.

▲ Musical instruments used in ancient Nubia are still played today.

In actuality, ancient Nubia was not a gateway so much as it was an historic avenue. Along the River Nile in Nubia, traders found a tremendous supply of ivory, gums, gold, and musical instruments. People came to Nubia from as far away as Punt (Somalia today) and the area of the Mountains of the Moon around Uganda and Zaire.

The Nubians were skilled in art, architecture, music, measurement, carving, and writing. Their script, called the Meroitic script, is still not completely understandable. It is clear, however, that the Nubians were an advanced culture for the time.

Scholars have called Nubia the *Avenue of Idea*s in the ancient world. Many of the important ideas and concepts that are thought of as Egyptian actually started in Nubia and traveled to Egypt. Among these ideas are the concepts of monarchy, or royal leadership, queenship, and totems. Throughout Africa people have found totems (animal or nature symbols) useful for cultural and spiritual identification. A *totem,* therefore, is the use of an animal or natural phenomenon to represent certain cultural beliefs.

Rule by one central leader who had legislative and executive powers seems to have begun in Nubia. Strong, central leaders made both decisions and laws in Nubia.

The first women leaders that we know about were among the Africans of Nubia. No other ancient civilization can boast of as many queens as Nubia. At one time, scholars thought that Nubia had been ruled by queens only. The kingdom of

Kush alone boasts 53 queens and 20 kings. We know most of the names of the Nubian queens. There is Queen Merniye of the 6th century B.C.E., Queen Batahaliye of the 4th century B.C.E., and Queen Shanakdakete who ruled between 170 B.C.E. and 150 B.C.E. African women ruled the greatest kingdoms of the Nile Valley. Truly, this country with its beautiful temples and fine cities was an avenue of ideas in many ways.

No major kingdom in the ancient world had as many women leaders as Nubia. The fact that Nubia gave the world the concepts of both monarchy and queenship suggests that the Nubians were comfortable with the idea as well as the reality of women in leadership positions. Indeed, they should not have had any problems with women leaders because women oversaw many of the building projects and military campaigns of the kingdom. Women could rule and lead the greatest kingdoms of the ancient world without loss of their credibility. Ancient Nubia, although it no longer exists, is still a living Avenue of Ideas for us. Our society can learn some lessons from the way women were treated in the ancient Nubian culture.

CENTER YOUR THINKING

1. Why was the ancient kingdom of Nubia known as a "child of the Nile"? Explain.

2. Describe the cataracts. Explain how the Nubians used the cataracts to their advantage.

3. **CRITICAL THINKING:** Do you think that Nubia should have been called The Avenue of History or The Avenue of Ideas in classical Africa? Why? Explain your answer.

CHAPTER

13 THE ROYAL LAND

PIANKHI

The first of the great Nubian kings was Piankhi. By all accounts, his conquest of Egypt was swift and powerful. It was also the first recorded conquest of Egypt. Some accounts say that he came down the Nile "like a cloudburst." Some say that he was "raging like a panther." His love of tradition inspired him to restore many temples and to return to the ancient religious ceremonies.

However, Piankhi's rule was strange in at least one way. After defeating Egypt, Piankhi did not remain there to rule. He chose to rule Egypt indirectly from Napata. When a rebellion broke out in the north of the country, Piankhi did not go himself. He sent his army to put down the revolt, but he did not lead them. We know the story of Piankhi's conquest because it is told on a giant stone stela at the temple of Amen at Gebel Barkal.

Piankhi was a very religious leader. The text written on the stone stelae says that he wished to avoid killing anyone if it was at all possible. It also said that all his opponents would be pardoned if they took a vow of loyalty to Piankhi. He is one of the first great conquerors in history to state categorically that he did not want to kill his enemies.

We also know that Piankhi loved animals. Piankhi personally scolded an Egyptian prince who let his horse starve during the war. He demanded horses as presents from the conquered Egyptians. When Piankhi died in 716 B.C.E., eight of his best horses were buried with him.

Chariots similar to ancient ones are still used today.

Piankhi's burial with horses suggests that he believed in the ancient Nile Valley religious idea of an eternal life after death in which people could enjoy pleasures from this world. This belief is found throughout the Nubian culture. Some kings buried their royal horses upright in graves made for four horses. These stand-up graves seemed to have been made for horses that pulled chariots, or ceremonial or military carriages.

TAHARKA

Taharka is mentioned in the Bible as one of the great kings of antiquity. He was the most distinguished pharaoh in the Nubian period. Taharka became king in 690 B.C.E. and ruled Nubia and Egypt until 664 B.C.E. Taharka was a proud king. Whenever he did something important, he wanted his relatives to know and appreciate what he had done.

Taharka's coronation as king shows his proud attitude. He arranged for his mother to travel almost 1,200 miles (1,935 kilometers) from Nubia to Memphis in the north of Egypt for his coronation. This is about as far as from New York to Chicago. She made the long trip to the ancient capital of northern Egypt and saw her son on the throne of Egypt. If she traveled 25 miles a day, how long would it have taken her? According to historical inscriptions, "...She rejoiced exceedingly after beholding the beauty of His Majesty Taharka...crowned upon the throne of Upper and Lower Egypt."

This magnificent sphinx was built by King Taharka.

In Pharaoh Taharka's reign, new building and restoration took place at an intense pace. Temples were restored, with gold and silver covers and faces added to the most holy sites. Many beautiful new sculptures were created and placed in public places.

Taharka also revived literature and poetry. One source tells a story about Taharka that demonstrates his personal style and temperament. According to the source,

Taharka once had his soldiers race through the desert at night for a distance of 30 miles (48 kilometers). This race was longer than our marathons, which are 26 (42 kilometers) miles. Taharka's race took five hours. He rode alongside the runners on horseback. Then, at the end of the race, he rewarded both winners and losers!

When Taharka's tomb was excavated, researchers found more than a thousand small statues called *shawabtis*. *Shawabtis* are funerary statuettes which are supposed to serve the dead person in the afterlife. A huge pyramid marks Taharka's burial place at Nuri.

▲ Small figures called *shawabtis* were believed to serve the dead in the afterlife.

ASPELTA

One of Taharka's great-grandsons was a king named Aspelta. He ruled from 600 B.C.E. to 580 B.C.E., after Nubia and Egypt had been defeated by the Assyrians. Aspelta's brother Anlamani ruled before him from 620 to 600 B.C.E., but Anlamani could not control the incursions, or small scale invasions, of other nations into the land.

Aspelta had long disputed his brother's accession to the throne and seemed eager to take the throne for himself, instead. Although there is not much historical evidence to tell us about Aspelta and Anlamani, it seems that Aspelta was the greater king.

One indication that Aspelta was greater is his tomb at Nuri. It contained a wealth of luxury items. Unlike many of the graves at the Nuri cemetery, Aspelta's was not completely robbed. Many works of art, precious metals, vases, and alabaster boxes were still in his tomb when it was found.

Aspelta seems to have been a powerful and wealthy king. But, like his brother Anlamani, his armies were eventually defeated by the Egyptians in 591 B.C.E. Aspelta was forced to withdraw from Napata back to Meroe.

WOMEN LEADERS IN KUSH

The role of women in ancient Kush was very important. The final decision about who would be king was often held by women. The custom, as in other African societies, was to pass the kingship to the child of a sister of the king. A brother could also become king, for example, Aspelta and Anlamani.

There were also many queens who ruled in the history of Nubia. Women as well as men were chosen. Women also held high positions because of the society's organization along matrilineal lines. "Mother of the King" and "Sister of the King" were important titles with great responsibility and power.

Nubians had great respect for the ability of women. At one point, the famous and important area of Thebes was placed under the control of a princess called the "God's Wife of Amen." This was a powerful religious title, and she had strong administrative powers in this position. In holding this office, the woman was considered to be married to the god Amen and not to a man.

QUEEN AMANITORE

The Kushite queen, Amanitore, lived about the time of Jesus, from 25 C.E. to 41 C.E. She ruled as queen in her own right. Her husband appears besides her in temple scenes, but he is never shown as a reigning king with any power. He is never shown without Amanitore. Amanitore was a descendant of a king, but her husband was not. She was buried in the great royal cemetery at Meroe while her husband was buried in an isolated place, away from the royal cemetery, indicating that he was not of the same rank as his wife. Although many scholars believe that Natakamani, the husband, helped organize the building program in Kush, he was not of the same stature as Amanitore; he was clearly beneath her.

The successor to Amanitore's rule was her son, Sherkarer. We believe that his reign was important, but that it did not exceed his mother's achievements.

NUBIAN QUEENS	
Bartare	284 - 275 B.C.E.
Shanakdakhete	177 - 155 B.C.E.
Amanerinas	99 - 84 B.C.E.
Amanishakete	26 - 20 B.C.E.
Amanitore	25 - 41 C.E.
Amanikhatashan	83 - 115 C.E.

CENTER YOUR THINKING

1. Tell about Pianki's contributions as a king of Nubia.

2. Compare the three Nubian kings described in this chapter. What contributions did each make to Nubian culture? In your opinion, which pharaoh had the greatest impact? Why?

3. Analyze the role of women leaders in Kush. Compare the roles of ancient Kushite women with the roles of women in our society today in the U.S. Tell some similarities as well as differences.

UNIT REVIEW

 ## SUMMARY

 The Nubian civilization, although sometimes called prehistoric because there is no written record that we understand, was quite an advanced culture. (p. 54)

 Physically and geographically, the land that was ancient Nubia has not changed much today. (p. 61)

 The Kushites valued the role of women and had many queens and high positions for women. (p. 68)

 Nubia and Egypt interacted as equals. Many of the ideas that some scholars had attributed to Egypt seem, instead, to have originated in Nubia, for example, the idea of a monarchy, royalty, queenship, totem and an of afterlife similar to physical life on earth. (pp. 55, 64, 67)

 The creativity of the ancient Africans is exemplified by the ancient Nubians in their strategy for using the six major cataracts of the Nile to their advantage. The Nubians set up a long string of villages all along the Nile, maintaining communication with each other and keeping watch for invading enemies. (pp.62-63)

Taharka's African attitude of pride in his achievements was exceeded only by that of his mother, who traveled almost 1,935 kilometers to attend her son's coronation as king. (pp. 67)

PERSONAL WITNESSING

REFLECTION

Imagine that you are an architect designing a memorial to ancient African leaders. What kind of structure would you like to build? Which leader would you choose? Why? What types of buildings would you like to design? What material would they be built of -- concrete, sand, marble, etc? How will your African memorial be different from Mount Rushmore? Write your ideas down.

TESTIMONY

Draw or build models of your own design for a memorial to the outstanding ancient African leader(s) you admire most. Put together a description, either oral or written, telling why you chose the leader(s) you did, what qualities you admire most, and how the memorial you have designed shows those qualities. What makes your memorial distinctly *African*?

"Follow in the footsteps of your ancestors, for the mind is trained through knowledge."

— Maulana Karenga

AXUM: THE GEM OF AFRICA

The Axumite kingdom was the most dominant empire on the horn of Africa for hundreds of years.

CENTER YOURSELF

King Ezana I of Axum left the language and culture of the Beja people intact when he conquered them. Was he a wise African ruler or a weak conqueror? Compare your attitudes with his. Would it have been better if Axum had not fought the Beja? What can be learned from Axum's dramatic story of rise and fall?

This 70-foot-tall monolith was erected in Axum during Africa's iron age.

CHAPTER

14 GLORIOUS AXUM

VOCABULARY
scholar

CENTER YOUR VOCABULARY

multicultural
multiethnic
gateway
Dawning
Glowing
Brilliant

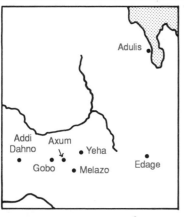

▲ Map of Axum

AXUM ARISES IN GRANDEUR

While the Meroitic kingdom was growing in strength and splendor, the Axum Expire was also gaining power. The Axum Empire arose around 220 C.E. in the African country which is called Ethiopia today. Axum, like Egypt, grew up around a river, the Tekezze River. The Blue Nile starts in Ethiopia. As a powerful nation, Axum would conquer the rest of Kush around 320-350 C.E.

The city of Adulis was one of the earliest centers of power in the Axum Empire. Known for the beauty of its official residences, public buildings, and the wealth of its citizens, the ancient city of Adulis was the multicultural and multiethnic symbol of Axum's political and military importance. Adulis was trading with Egypt during the reign of the Ptolemaic kings, the Greek rulers of Egypt, for almost three-hundred years (333 B.C.E. to 50 B.C.E.) Although we do not know for sure, it is entirely possible that Egypt and Axum were trading and knew each other even earlier. Travel was fairly easy and frequent up and down the Red Sea between Axum and Egypt.

Much older cities than Adulis had existed and become famous in the Axum Empire, although none were so glorious. Two earlier cities had come to fame in the time just before the Axum Empire became great. These were Yeha and Kaskase. Both cities had been centers of influence and trade. These two ancient towns go way back in history, and African history is some of the oldest. We have no specific dates for Yeha's and Kaskase's origin. We know that they existed as viable communities as early as 2000 B.C.E., but no one knows the precise dates of their origin.

Like many other ancient African civilizations, the Axumites wrote down important things. Today, we have learned much from their writings. They wrote about their religion, about their kings, and about their feelings.

The ancient writings of the Axumite Empire tell their story in fascinating detail. Stones were found in the country with writings in several languages, like the Rosetta stone. From the stones we have learned that the Axumite scholars knew several different ancient languages, including Ge'ez, the ancient language of Axum; Greek; the language of the Egyptian Christian Church; and an Arabic dialect from South Arabia. A *dialect* is a regional or local version of a major language. For example, people in Brooklyn, New York, may be said to speak an American English dialect.

In addition to the writings of ancient Axum, we have many Axumite artifacts that reveal a powerfully artistic civilization. The ancient Axumite obelisks rival those of Kemet and Nubia as do the stelae, altars, throne bases, and other large stone structures.

If you close your eyes and try to imagine the grandeur of the Axum Empire with its copper coins, objects of bronze, ironworks, precious stones, pottery, gold, glass, and ceramics all spread out before you, the image that you will have is only a pale copy of the original.

A large part of the grandeur of Axum was in its use of these grand objects for religious and ceremonial purposes. Iron was used to make utensils for religious celebrations as well as for everyday use at home. But of all the magnificent Axumite objects we can examine today, the pottery tells us more about how the Axumite people thought of themselves and their world. Different people decorate their pottery in different ways that show their viewpoint. It was said of them as it has been said of other Africans, "By their pottery, you know them."

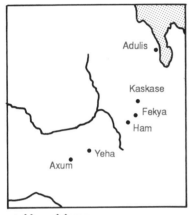
▲ Map of Axum

▲ Drawing of a human-headed jar from the Tomb of the Brick Arches

HISTORICAL PERIODS OF ANCIENT AXUM
THE DAWNING STAGE
499 B.C.E. - 399 B.C.E.

I have named this first period the *Dawning Stage* because the Axumite Empire was rising, just beginning to dawn. The Dawning Stage lasted from the end of the 5th century B.C.E. to the end of the 4th century B.C.E.

Less is known about this early stage than about later periods in the development of the Axumite Empire. It may have been during the Dawning Stage that Africans crossed the Red Sea to southern Arabia and influenced the Arabian culture in Yemen.

In fact, the evidence suggests that the ancient people of the southern region of Arabia resembled the Africans in appearance and skin color. Many people today cannot tell the difference between a Yemenite and an Ethiopian by looking at them. When the two talk, of course, their languages are different enough that they cannot understand each other.

Evidence of interactions between these two cultures is intense. The architecture at Yeha clearly shows some of the same influences found in Arabia. Sculptures at Haoulti-Melazo are extremely similar to ones found in Arabia. Undoubtedly, the interaction was social as well as artistic and went both ways, from culture to culture, during this period.

▲ The architecture of churches in Lalibela (Ethiopia today) is similar to that in Arabia.

THE GLOWING STAGE
201 B.C.E. - 99 C.E.

A second stage extends from the beginning of the 3rd century B.C.E. to the end of the 1st century C.E. and the start of Christianity. The interaction with southern Arabia, especially the coast of southern Arabia, becomes weaker due to Axum's concentration on its own internal problems. At the same time, the relationship between Axum and Egypt grows stronger because of the Ptolemaic quest for greater involvement with African states. I have called this stage the *Glowing Stage* because the Axumite Empire came into its own strength during this period.

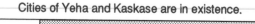

Cities of Yeha and Kaskase are in existence.

Little is known about the earliest days of Axum before 2000 B.C.E.

2000
B.C.E.

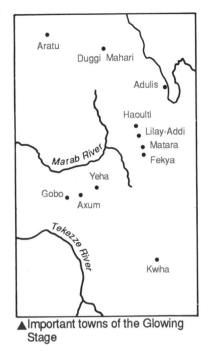

▲Important towns of the Glowing Stage

The pottery of this period is impressive. But magnificent ironwork and bronze artifacts are also found in ancient Axum at this time.

Some Important Historical Towns of the Glowing Stage	
Yeha	trading and commercial center
Li'Lay-Addi	textile and perfume center
Gobo-Fench	timber center
Haoulti	hunting center
Matara	bronze and iron center
Fekya	religious center

These were among the most vigorous towns in all of Africa. People came to them to trade, discover what was new, meet friends, and hear the latest political stories.

During the Glowing Stage, the port city of Adulis became Axum's main gateway to the world. In addition, scholars have found 60 different inscriptions, or writings, on the ancient buildings in Axum. These inscriptions suggest that Axum was actively engaged in communication with other people and in recording historical events and ceremonial and memorial writings. Developments in art and agriculture meant Axum was ready for a new, more expansive influence on the world.

THE BRILLIANT STAGE 100 C.E. - 899 C.E.

The period of history in which Axum's power and culture explodes into greatness is what I call the *Brilliant Stage* from the first century C.E. to the end of the 9th century C.E. The ancient African civilization of Axum was in full glory during this time.

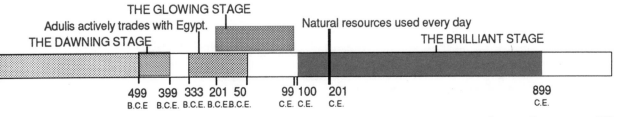

Evidence of Axum's brilliance during this period is everywhere, in all fields. Axum was the most advanced civilization during this time in the northeastern part of Africa. Some of the wisest people who had lived and the most respected works had come from Axum in many fields, such as writing, language, religion, statesmanship, and government. With the assistance of a bureaucracy knowledgeable about the Greek and Egyptian languages as well as other languages of trade, Axum practiced the best forms of government. It was a disciplined state based on order, justice, and harmony.

By the Brilliant Stage, the distinctively different culture of Axum was alive! Its culture and character was its own, not a replay of Nubia or Egypt, its rivals in Africa. High in the Ethiopian plateau, the Axumites produced outstanding works of bronze, iron, and ivory. Axum was the most important city of the kingdom. It was a journey of eight days overland from the seaport of Adulis. By the Brilliant Stage, Axum was resplendent in riches, having conquered the empire of Nubia and consolidated its wealth.

Although Axum's public buildings were square or rectangular like those of Nubia and Egypt, they still had their own peculiar Axumite style of architecture. The foundations of the Axumite buildings appeared to have tiers or floors that alternated in projecting outward and recessing inward.

▲ This limestone temple at Yeha was 50 feet tall. The blocks are held together with no cement!

The Axumites, like other ancient Africans, created buildings to express their faith in their religion and their belief in the grandeur of their kingdom. Axumite buildings were often built in huge, monolithic dimensions and spaces. Most Axumite buildings were made of granite. The granite was similar to the Aswan granite of which the obelisks in Egypt were made.

Among the important architectural achievements of Axum during this stage were Kaleb's tomb at Axum and the Giant Stelae, both meant to be funerary monuments to the kings.

Cities of Yeha and Kaskase are in existence.

Little is known about the earliest days of Axum before 2000 B.C.E.

2000
B.C.E.

These massive structures are elaborately carved and showed repetition of characteristically African aesthetic designs. Other sites with cities of importance include Ham, Mekalli, Tokonda, Kohaito, Aratou, Adua, and, of course, the seaport, Adulis.

During this period, public writing seems to have flourished, too. By public writing is meant official decrees, descriptions of wars and conquests, dedications to deities and ceremonial liturgies, and praises in writing. In its public form, this writing appeared everywhere. Almost every public building, stela, obelisk, and throne base seems to have had a written inscription. Modern day tourists certainly would gain the impression that the Axumites were prolific writers.

By the third century C.E., the Axumites began to use natural resources for everyday purposes. Gold, silver, and bronze were used to make coins throughout the empire. Unlike the Egyptians and Nubians who did not make much use of coins, the Axumites perfected the use of coins in external trade. Their internal trade also used bronze coins, but they relied heavily on the system of bartering. Axumite potters began to make pottery in new shapes and colors that were both beautifully decorated and functional.

Axum was a magnet for ideas. People came to the country from afar to trade. Axumites were in contact with the world. In fact, numerous visitors came to Axum to learn and to study at the feet of its growing intellectual class. One Greek visitor, Cosmas Indicopleutes, wrote that he found "everywhere in Axum and Adulis churches of Christians, bishops, martyrs, monks, and recluses by whom the Gospel of Christ is proclaimed." Thus in the 6th century C.E., Axum was a seat of the Christian religion which urged believers to *go into all the world.*" Indeed, in the late 9th century C.E., Al-Yaqubi wrote that there were *"mighty cities of the Abyssinians visited by Arab merchants of Dahlak.*"

▲ Drawing of an Axumite coin

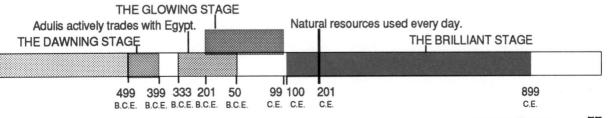
THE GLOWING STAGE
Adulis actively trades with Egypt.
THE DAWNING STAGE

Natural resources used every day.
THE BRILLIANT STAGE

| 499 | 399 | 333 | 201 | 50 | 99 | 100 | 201 | 899 |
| B.C.E. | B.C.E. | B.C.E. | B.C.E. | B.C.E. | C.E. | C.E. | C.E. | C.E. |

CHAPTER

15 AXUM'S GIFTS TO THE WORLD

THROUGH AFRICA INTO AXUM

Ancient Axum was connected by land to Kemet and to Nubia. Furthermore, one branch of the River Nile, the Abay, which flows into the Mediterranean Sea, starts in the highlands of Ethiopia. From the interior of Ethiopia to the Mediterranean Sea there is a waterway that connects Axum to Nubia and Egypt linking the three great civilizations of northeastern Africa.

For some reason that I do not understand, some historians in the past tried to show that the Egyptians and others interacted with the Axumites without ever going through or into any other part of Africa. On your map, trace a line from Axum to Kemet with your finger. Do you pass through Nubia? Can you get to Kemet without going through Nubia? It seems impossible and illogical to me.

Now find the cities of Axum and Yeha on the map. These two cities are in the western part of the ancient empire, away from the sea. What might you hypothesize about reaching them?

The same construction techniques and methods of building that were used in Kemet and Nubia were also being used in Axum. Even the reliefs, or carved pictures, on the walls of temples and other buildings are similar. It seems to be stretching the truth to believe that Axum, Kemet, and Nubia were not interacting across Africa.

Could you travel conveniently to Kemet from Axum without going through Nubia? ▼

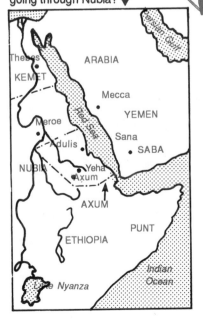

The ways the Axumites, Egyptians, and Nubians put stones together to build were almost identical. The use of pillars and columns of stone had, of course, long been an African practice. However, in Axum it becomes a practice employed on a vast monumental scale, often for Christian churches and tombs of kings.

The Axumite Empire had houses for the nobles and elite that were mansions or like palaces in size. In the cities of Axum and Matara, there are ruins of these palaces that still stand today. These elaborate villas are of the highest artistic quality. They reflect attention to detail and design representative of Axum's glory during its years of pre-eminence as an African empire. The Axumite palaces are at least as elaborate and grand in both scale and quality as any architecture of the time.

The idea of the house complex in Axum probably came from the idea of the compound in African societies, where separate buildings serving various functions are connected

▲ The architecture in ancient Axum resembles that of castles and other structures of the same period in Europe.

by a common courtyard or walled-in walkways to show relationship. Thus, a family might use one small building for storage, another for sleeping, another for guests, another for entertainment, and so forth. In the United States we tend to have all functions of the family under one roof.

The civilization of Axum flourished, making its own important and unique contributions to art, architecture, and religion. At the same time, Axum was engaged in international trade with China, Persia, Sri Lanka, Arabia, and India. With the Red Sea port of Adulis as its gateway to the world, Axum firmly established its network of commerce with other nations.

The sophisticated Axumite civilization has not been studied as much as Kemet and Nubia, but, in recent years, research into Axum has intensified for anyone interested in the study of classical Africa. Although we do not yet know all of Axum's many contributions, their advanced styles of architecture and ceramics are particularly impressive.

The Axumite Kingdom is also rich in historical lore and legend. One story that is told is that the Queen of Sheba lived in Axum. Another story is that she had a son with King Solomon. Another story has it that one of the holiest places in ancient Axum was the Gabaza Axum, which held the Jewish Ark of the Covenant. It was said to have been moved from Jersusalem by King Menelik. No one knows yet if these stories are fact or fiction, but we do know that ancient Axum was far greater than any of the stories that remain.

CENTER YOUR THINKING

1. What two bodies of water connected the lands of the Axumite, Nubian, and Egyptian empires?

2. Tell some ways in which the great Axumite, Nubian, and Egyptian civilizations interacted with each other. Why must these interactions have occurred? Explain some issues that might have affected all three empires.

3. CRITICAL THINKING: Give your own evaluation of ancient Axum's artistic achievements. How do "ruins" help scholars infer, or make well-educated guesses, about the achievements of a civilization? What do you infer about ancient Axum from its ruins?

CHAPTER

16 THE POWER OF AXUM

VOCABULARY

protectorate intermediary
coastline

Center Your Vocabulary

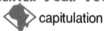 capitulation

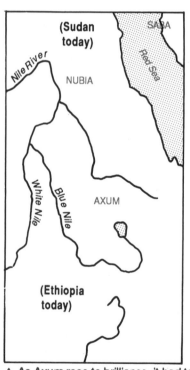

▲ As Axum rose to brilliance, it had to deal with its neighbors, Nubia and Saba, who were in decline.

The Brilliant Stage, 100 C.E. - 899 C.E.

Axum rose to its brilliance about the same time as Rome. But two important neighbors of Axum, Nubia in Africa and Saba in Arabia, were now in decline.

Nubia had controlled the Nile, and Saba had controlled much of the Red Sea. Axum's rise, indeed, at the expense of Nubia and Saba changed the political equation and impacted Rome's power. Rome was dependent on the support of Nubia and Saba and had extended its trade into the northeast of Africa and southern Arabia.

Because of the decline of Nubia and Saba in the 4th century C.E., Axum would later have to help Rome protect its ships in the Red Sea against pirates. Axum would also stop the Beja ethnic groups from attacking the south of Egypt, which was now a protectorate, or territory under the political control of Rome. Since the capitulation of Egypt during the rule of the Greek-descended Queen Cleopatra in 50 B.C.E., the Romans had steadily increased their presence in eastern African affairs.

Axum, as the mightiest of the nations in the area in the 4th century C.E., exercised authority over politics and commercial activities in the region.

By controlling the entire Red Sea, Axum controlled the sea trade between Africa and Asia. By the time Axum entered the Brilliant Stage in 100 C.E., Africans from Axum were trading

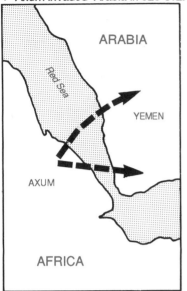
▼ Axum invaded Arabia in 528 C.E.

with Asians from India, Sri Lanka, and China. When Axum reached eastward to take control of the sea lanes, it became a middle or intermediary power, a force to be dealt with between Asia and the people of the Mediterranean Sea region.

Axum protected the trade ships that stopped at ports along the shore of Somalia, ancient Punt, and Ethiopia. In the ancient world, Axum was famous as the protector of trading ships along this coastline. Often, pirates from Arabia and the coast of Africa would wait until a ship put to shore. Then the pirates would attack and steal the goods from the ship.

As the Axum Empire gained power, it put an end to this kind of piracy. Many people were grateful because this type of piracy had been a common, almost everyday occurrence that dogged the ships on the Red Sea.

The Axum Empire invaded Arabia in 528 C.E. and ruled the Yemenite area of the Arabian Peninsula until 575 C.E. The military and political might of the Axum Empire was so great that its neighbors, such as Meroe and Sennar, paid taxes and gave gifts to the Axumite ruler.

Thus, Axum, first described in the book *Periplus of the Erythraeans* written in the 2nd century C.E., as "a place to which all the ivory is brought from the countries beyond the Nile" sparkled as a brilliant gem in the history of classical Africa.

CENTER YOUR THINKING

1. Why did Axum and Rome become friends and allies? How did this friendship help Rome? Why did some people in the Mediterranean region see Axum as their protector?

2. Explain how you know that Axum was a powerful military force in ancient Africa. Give at least two reasons.

3. **CRITICAL THINKING:** Explain what the following statement says about the Empire of Axum:

   "Axum is a place to which all the ivory is brought from the countries beyond the Nile."

CHAPTER

17 THE CONQUEST OF THE LAND

VOCABULARY
flesh
CENTER YOUR VOCABULARY

subjugate
subject

THE MILITARY POWER OF AXUM

Axum was a great military power, able to defeat most of the armies in Africa and Arabia. In one inscription, the king of the Adulis area reports:

> "HAVING COMMANDED THE PEOPLES CLOSEST TO MY KINGDOM TO PRESERVE THE PEACE, I BRAVELY WAGED WAR AND SUBJUGATED IN BATTLES THE FOLLOWING PEOPLES...."

The king then gives a long list of nations that his army has defeated. Included in the list of countries defeated by the armies of Axum was a land called Sennar. It was located near the Blue Nile River (the Abay) and had become a major source of irritation to the Axumites, attacking them on the borders of the Axum Empire. Another country in the list of nations is described as a land of "high mountains, cold winds, and mist." For Axum to have defended such a nation in Africa, it would have had to travel as far as central Ethiopia, Kenya, or Uganda. These areas are known for their mountains, mist, and sometimes cold weather.

To win their military campaigns, the armies of Axum had to travel to the south, the southwest, and the north. To be able to organize such long, complex travel, the political and military leaders of Axum must have been incredibly capable. What kind of preparation would these soldiers have had to make? They traveled to hot climates as well as cold. If you did not know that there were cold climates in Africa, you may want to learn more on your own about Kenya and Tanzania.

During periods of conquest and expansion, the Axumite kings ordered that stelae, obelisks, and other monuments be built. They wanted to show their power in the area. Similarly, the king of Axum had a monument built in the city of Adulis on the Red Sea as a sign of his authority to rule the entire region.

The conquering king, whose name we do not know, says in an inscription on a stela in Axum that he defeated all of his neighbors in the surrounding territories. In fact, he did more than defeat all the people who lived on the border with Egypt. He "...again made the road from Egypt to Axum a thoroughfare." By a *thoroughfare,* he probably meant a way through which considerable human traffic passed. What do you think he might have meant by *again* in this inscription?

By the 3rd century C.E., the Axum Empire was firmly established as one of the great empires of the ancient world. Again, the public buildings of the Axumites reflected this greatness. Between 270 and 320 C.E., the greatest of the monolithic structures of ancient Axum, the Cyclopean stone monument, had been built. Throne bases, obelisks, and stelae showing important events dotted the empire.

The Iranian prophet, Mani, who lived from 216 to 276 C.E. and was the founder of Manicheism, a belief that all flesh is evil, wrote in a book called *The Chapters* that there were four great empires in the world. He named them as the Persian Empire, the Roman Empire, the Axumite Empire, and the Chinese Empire.

The Axumite Empire, like other ancient empires such as the Persian and Roman empires, began to mint, or make their own coins, in the 3rd century C.E. Coins had been used in Africa before, so it was probably only a matter of time before the Axumite Empire did the same.

▲ This Axumite monolith shows the monumentality of such structures.

▼ Drawing of an ancient
Axumite coin

By making its own money, Axum could control the supply of money in its empire. Only the government of the Axum Empire had the authority to issue gold, silver, and copper coins within its kingdoms.

In contrast, the Persians and Romans issued only silver or copper coins. The Persians and Romans let the rulers of the kingdoms they controlled issue gold coins in addition to the Persian and Roman coins of silver and copper. In this way, the Persians and Romans sometimes lost control of the money supply to the kings they had conquered.

THE MANY FACES OF ETHIOPIA

The Axumite Empire has often been called Ethiopia. However, *Ethiopia* was also used as a general term for Africa in ancient times.

The word *Aethiopica,* from which we get *Ethiopia,* is a Greek word meaning "burnt faces." To the Greeks, the dark skin of the Africans appeared to be burnt. However, the Africans, understandably, did not see themselves as being "burnt." They simply called themselves either Axumites or Abyssinians. The word *Abyssinia* corresponds to the Arabic, *Habesha.*

One good source of information about the Axum Empire is the Greek writer Heliodorus's historical novel, *Aethiopica,* written around 280-300 C.E. The setting of the novel is the time of Persian control over Egypt. In the novel, Nubia (Meroe) is described as being at the height of its power. Also in the novel, triumphal celebrations occur often in which nations that have been conquered must walk past the king for him to see what he has conquered.

One thing that is interesting in the novel is that all of the nations that paid tribute to Nubia and passed before the eyes of the king had to bow before the king. They knelt, and some actually fell completely on the ground, before the king, to show that they were subject to his authority.

However, the king of Axum remained upright, not bowing, paying no tribute to the Nubian king. Appearing at the very last before the Nubian king, the Axumite king expressed friendship with the Nubians.

In this novel, the Axumites are shown as equals to the Nubians, whom they would later supersede. Unfortunately, for Nubia, as it grew weaker, Axum grew stronger. Finally, around 290 C.E., the king of Axum invaded Nubia and added it to his empire. In fact, the last king of Meroe whose name we know, Teceridamani, does not even appear in historical records after 254 C.E. And we know that there were six more kings after him. The additional six kings remain anonymous, and perhaps we will never know their names. Their names are worn off the stone stele.

CENTER YOUR THINKING

1. Why do you think the Axumite armies were so powerful? Give at least two reasons and explain your thinking.

2. Compare and contrast the Axumite, Roman, and Persian empires' use of coins. Which economic or barter system do you feel was best? Why?

3. CRITICAL THINKING: In the novel *Aethiopica* by the Greek writer Heliodorus, the Axumites are presented as the equals of the Nubians. In the novel, Nubia grows weaker and is conquered by Axum. If you were king or queen of Axum, why might you have wanted to invade Nubia and conquer it? Why might you have decided not to invade Nubia and conquer it? Explain your answer.

CHAPTER

18 EZANA I: THE WISE KING

VOCABULARY
paramount   supremacy

CENTER YOUR VOCABULARY

tradition
resettlement

WISE, GREAT, AND FAMOUS

The first king of Axum of whom we have written records from both inside and outside of Axum was Ezana I. The reigns of most ancient kings were written about only by those inside their own countries. In the case of Ezana I, we have an Axumite king who was known far and wide -- in Rome, Greece, Arabia, Egypt, and India!

The writer Rufinus tells us in his 6th century *Ecclesiastical History* that a Syrian Christian while traveling to India with his two sons, Aedesius and Frumentius, was shipwrecked off the coast of Axum during the reign of King Ella Amida, the father of Ezana I. Ella Amida adopted the two young boys and put them in the service of his son, Ezana. When the young man became king, he brought Aedesius and Frumentius to his court as advisors.

King Ezana I was the paramount king of a large empire that included Axum, Arabia, Saba, Abyssinia, Beja, and Meroe. Few kings in ancient times could have found a more powerful group of nations to rule. The whole region that included all these countries was later called Axum.

As great as Ezana I was, he still followed in the traditions of the kings of Nubia and Egypt in at least one way. He still fought the Beja people who lived in the desert.

The Beja were a proud, dignified people who were used to being free and independent. They usually refused to pay taxes to any other nation. For this reason, they fought with many different empires.

Ezana I, however, succeeded in conquering them without going to battle himself. Instead, he sent his two brothers, She'azana and Hadefa, to head the Axumite army during the middle of the 4th century C.E. At the end of the battle with the Beja people, the Beja knew that they would have to recognize the supremacy of Axum.

After the Axumite brothers had won, they made the six Beja kings and many of the Beja people, along with their cattle, walk to the court of Ezana I at Axum. The migration from the land of the Beja to the court of Ezana took four long months because it involved all of the royal houses of Beja, the royal wives, children, and animals!

Upon arriving in Axum, this large group of Beja people, now Axumite subjects, bowed to the Axumite king. Ezana I could have killed them or punished them. But his mercy and generosity knew no bounds. Ezana I let the Beja keep their families together, their animals, their language, and their ethnic and cultural traditions.

Such was Ezana's respect for the Beja that he did everything he could to assist them except, of course, to allow them the freedom to disrupt trade routes. Thus, the resettlement of the Beja was to anticipate many more removals of the people. In the 20th century, the Beja, Nuba, and Nubians have been resettled because of war and technology. The most memorable example of the resettlement of thousands of Beja and Nubians occurred during the building of the Aswan High Dam in Egypt.

Attempting to show respect for the Beja, Ezana commanded his officers not to interfere with the Bejas. In addition to this gesture, Ezana I ordered that 25,000 long-horned cattle, clothing, and food be given to the Beja kings.

There was great rejoicing in Axum. The Beja, now weakened by their four-month journey, could not plan a rebellion for a long time. We will never know if Ezana I was just cunning and clever or if he was truly a wise and forgiving leader. What do you think?

An inscription written with the authority of Ezana I says:

> "REBELLIOUS PEOPLE WERE SUBDUED,
> RENOUNCING PROLONGED STRUGGLE.
> THE KING RESETTLED THEM
> AT ENORMOUS DISTANCE."

Gifts were brought to Ezana I by the people he had defeated. The defeated nations remembered the names of the gods of Axum: Astar, Beher, and Medr. And when they came to pay respect to the king, they remembered that the chief god of his family had been Mahrem before the coming of Christianity, and therefore most of the nations presented their gifts of gold, silver, and bronze to Ezana in Mahrem's name.

But Ezana ruled a country that was becoming increasingly Christian although he respected the older, traditional cultures of Africa.

By the time Ezana I died around 357 C.E., Frumentius and Aedesius had begun to exercise administrative and intellectual influence on the country. Thus, while they had been given as servants to Ezana by his father, Ella Amida, they had succeeded in becoming important players in the government of Axum.

At the death of Ezana I, the young men regained their freedom but chose to remain in Axum to serve the new king, Ezana II, who was about 13 years old at the time. However, when Ezana II became 18 years old Frumentius and Aedesius left Axum and went to Alexandria, whereupon Aedesius became an important citizen and Frumentius was appointed bishop of Africa by the patriarch Athanasius.

CENTER YOUR THINKING

1. List the five large nations ruled by King Ezana I of Axum. How did Axum's leadership make it a strong military nation? What would you have suggested to King Ezana I to make him an even better king?

2. Who were the Beja people? Explain how the Beja were a constant frustration to the other major classical societies of Africa.

3. **CRITICAL THINKING:** When the Beja were conquered, how did they come to the Axumite capital? Explain the difference between being abject and being proud. Which best describes the Beja? Why do you think that the Axumites decided not to humiliate the Beja people as they had humiliated other people they had conquered?

UNIT REVIEW

SUMMARY

 The grandeur and advanced culture of the Axumite Empire is evidenced in many ways, including their copper coinage, bronze art, ceramics, and the grandeur of their architecture, which they used to express their deep religious faith and their achievements. (pp. 73, 76)

 The Axumite armies were highly advanced in military leadership, strategies, and training, as evidenced by their ability to wage successful military campaigns throughout Africa in climates ranging from freezing cold to the desert. (p. 85)

 The similarities and interactions among Kemet, Nubia, and Axum are too striking to dismiss, as some historians have. Egyptians must have traveled through Africa to reach Nubia. And the striking similarity in physical appearance, including skin color, of Yemenites and Ethiopians today suggests that these cultures interacted long ago. (pp. 74, 79)

 The ancient Axumites left many writings, and they expressed their feelings about such universal topics as their religious beliefs and their king. (p. 73)

 Perhaps the most advanced achievement of any Axumite king was the compassion and wisdom of Ezana I, who did not humiliate the Beja people when he defeated them, but allowed them to maintain their customs and culture, a relevant lesson in wisdom for today. (p. 89)

 The respectful attitude of the ancient world toward Axum is evidenced in the novel *Aethiopica* by Heliodorus. All other nations bowed in tribute before the conquering Nubians except one -- Axum. (p. 86)

PERSONAL WITNESSING

REFLECTION

The ancient city of Adulis was multicultural and multiethnic, just as our society is today. Think about the problems and benefits the ancient people might have experienced as a result, both politically and socially. How might the ancient people of Adulis resolved some of their cultural and ethnic conflicts? How does our society today compare with theirs? What do you think can be learned from the changes and developmental stages Adulis went through?

TESTIMONY

According to the author, Dr. Asante, ancient Axum's Brilliant Stage was the historical period when its power and culture were at their greatest point. Do you feel that the United States has reached its Brilliant Stage? Why? What events in U.S. history have signaled changes in its development? Why? How do multicultural issues and the contributions of African Americans and Africans play a part in the development of the U.S.? Explain your thinking to the class.

> *"The only thing that is new is that which has been forgotten."*
> — Charles Finch

GHANA: THE KINGDOM OF IVORY AND GOLD

Ghana is the earliest major kingdom to rise in West Africa. It is the first of the great Sudanic empires.

CENTER YOURSELF

A contemporary African country bears the name of the ancient Empire of Ghana. Why do you think the founders of modern Ghana chose this classical name for their country? Research the name *Kwame Nkrumah*. Where did he attend college? Why is he considered the modern father of Ghana?

This intricately beautiful ivory carving is from Benin, West Africa.

CHAPTER
19 THE WEALTH OF GHANA

VOCABULARY

sahel   pavilion

CENTER YOUR VOCABULARY

traditional
duba

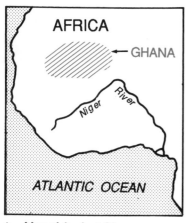

▲ Map of Ancient Ghana

OF THE OLDEST AND GREATEST KINGDOMS

The kingdoms of West Africa are among the oldest African kingdoms we know of, dating from about 1000 B.C.E. They can be studied in several ancient sources. Between the time of the fall of Axum in the 4th century C.E. and the appearance of written records about the West African kingdoms or states in the 8th century C.E. is a period of about four hundred years.

The earliest written records of the states in West Africa are Arabic sources. In 738 C.E., the writer Wahb ibn Munabbeh listed the people of the Sudan region as the Goran near Lake Chad, the Zaghawa in western Darfur, the Habesha of Abyssinia, the Qibt, which is actually Copts, and the Barbar or Berber. More information about West Africa appears in a famous book called *Meadows of Gold and Mines of Gems*. It was written in 947 C.E. by the geographer Al-Masudi of Baghdad. The book is now famous and tells of the Beja, Nubians, Zanj, and others who traveled to the southern portions of Africa.

The kingdoms of West Africa were listed as among the greatest of their time by Al-Masudi, Wahb ibn Munabbeh and others. The West African kingdoms of this period are Ghana,

Ghana

Mali   Songhay

300 BCE

1200 CE   1350 CE   1600 CE

300 B.C.E. to 1200 C.E.; Mali, 1200 C.E. to 1500 C.E.; and Songhay, 1350 C.E. to 1600 C.E.

The outstanding African historian, Abdurrahman Es-Sadi, who was born in 1596 C.E. in the city of Timbuktu, wrote the book *Tarikh es Sudan (History of the Sudan)*. He says in this book that a town on the Niger River near the city of Gao flourished at the same time as the 18th dynasty in ancient Egypt. The city of Burrum, a little town near Gao, was said to be one of the residences of the pharaohs.

Today, we call this kingdom early Ghana. However, strictly speaking, the name *Ghana* was the title given to the kings of the land. The kingdom of Wagadu that we call Ghana today rose as an important political and cultural empire about 300 B.C.E. Ghana is in a region covering most of the modern countries of Mali, parts of Senegal, Guinea, Morocco, and Mauritania. Because the area is mostly *sahel*, or dry, semi-desert region, the kingdom of Ghana made great use of the horse for war, travel, and work. Had Ghana been a forest empire, travel by horse would have given way to travel by foot.

THE GHANAIAN KING

The writer, Al-Bakri, gives a close-up look at the kingdom of Ghana in a book written around 1068 C.E. Al-Bakri traveled to Ghana. He found that the king of Ghana, just like the kings of West African traditional nations today, adorned himself with gold bracelets, necklaces, and a beautiful hat. The king wore the finest clothes of cotton decorated with gold from the Ghanaian gold mines.

▼A drawing of an ancient Ghanaian king, Tenkamenin

The king's palace was stunning, with gold everywhere. Ten horses covered with gold-embroidered cloths stood outside the living area. Behind the king stood ten pages holding shields and swords decorated with gold. The sons of lesser kings stood to the right of the Ghanaian king. They wore the beautiful costumes of their people and had their hair braided with gold.

The king was a leader and a judge. He sat under a domed pavilion and heard cases against members of his government. The king's decisions were considered to be the law of the land.

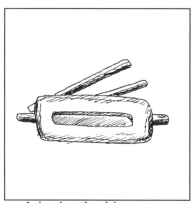

▲ A drawing of a *duba*

When the king wanted to speak, make an announcement or call a group together, he first called for the drummer. The king's drummer beat the *duba*, a massive drum made from a long hollow tree trunk. Without the *duba,* the people could not come together and the king could not speak.

Al-Bakri's account says that the mayor of the city sat on the ground before the king. The king was surrounded by his ministers, who also sat on the ground. Most likely, they sat on handwoven mats or rugs.

The king was guarded by dogs of excellent pedigree, or breeding. The royal dogs never took their eyes off the king. Even the dogs had collars of gold and silver studded with gold and silver balls.

In the 11th century when Al-Bakri saw the king of Ghana, the king practiced a traditional African religion. When people went to visit the king, they fell on their knees and sprinkled dust on their heads. This was a custom that showed deep respect for the king, who was the embodiment of the entire nation. No person could stand before the king as an equal.

Al-Bakri's impression of the ancient kingdom of Ghana was amazingly clear, perceptive, and accurate. Without a doubt, we know today that Ghana was one of the great classical cultures of ancient Africa.

CENTER YOUR THINKING

1. List two ancient sources for studying the empires of ancient Africa. Did you first learn of these sources in this book or in other studies of yours?

2. Tell at least two ways in which the kings of ancient Ghana used natural resources to their own advantage.

3. CRITICAL THINKING: Tell some different ways that gold was used in ancient Ghana. Do you think these were the best uses for this natural resource? Explain your opinion.

CHAPTER

20 THE GOLD & SALT TRADE OF GHANA

▲ All the kings of Ghana, to this day, are adorned with a wealth of gold. This has been true since the 4th century C.E. The artist's drawing above shows how King Osei Tutu, who reigned from 1680 to 1717 C.E., might have looked in all his gold splendor.

TOTAL CONTROL OF TRADE

The Ghanaian Empire was one of the first West African empires to hold total control over the natural resources of the region. As a result, Ghana controlled trade, as well. They used this control to increase their wealth.

Ghana would not allow people from any other kingdom to travel across Ghana unless they paid a tax to the king of Ghana. If traders from the area of present day Guinea wanted to travel to Morocco and trade gold, they had to pay a tax to the king of Ghana. Anyone in the salt trade also paid a tax to the Ghanaian king. To be a salt trader, you had to take the salt from the northern mines down to the south to trade it. There was no way around Ghana and the taxes it collected.

No other king was as powerful, and no nation contested Ghana for supremacy from the 4th century B.C.E. to the 11th century C.E. Everyone from Morocco to the forest and from the ocean to the Niger River gave honor, and often paid taxes, to the Ghanaian Empire.

A KINGDOM OF GOLD IN THE DESERT

Gold was the most precious commodity or product controlled by the Ghanaians. For this reason the land is often referred to as the ancient "kingdom of gold." There was so much gold that the people traded only gold dust! The king owned all of the gold nuggets.

The fact that only the gold dust was available to the people for trade kept inflation in control, according to the writer and historian, Al-Bakri. Otherwise, everyone would have had so much gold that the prices would go sky high.

Inflation means that prices are high or rising above where they should be. With high inflation, your money buys less and is worth less.

Inflation can happen when money is readily available, but goods are not. Then the price of goods climbs higher and higher. Your money buys less and less. Because goods are hard to get, a person who has goods to sell can keep raising the price of the goods. For example, the price of bread in Russia tripled when the government printed money to satisfy the people's demand for reasonable wages. However, because goods were so scarce that they were almost unavailable, the situation became one in which a lot of money was chasing very few goods. The result was that the people who had the goods raised their prices extremely high!

Ghana tried to control inflation and the price of gold by letting the king own all the gold nuggets. Citizens could use only the gold dust for trade. This left the main gold reserves in the hands of the king. Al-Bakri said that this precaution was necessary so that gold would not become too plentiful and lose its value.

THE SALT OF GHANA

Traders came from the rest of Africa, Asia, and Europe to get salt as well as gold dust. People in Africa from the south wanted salt to eat. Salt was also used for spice and trade by Europeans and Asians. Solid blocks of salt could be bartered or traded for precious metals or food.

The sources of the gold and salt in Ghana were never revealed to the outside world during ancient times. The kingdom of Ghana served as the keeper of both gold and salt. The Ghanaians held tight control over the supply.

We now know that most of the Ghanaian salt came from ancient lake sites. There are hundreds of lake beds in West Africa where salt can be found. The salt was cut into huge

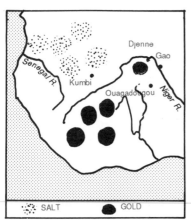

▲The areas in Ghana where gold (G) and salt (S) were mined are shown on this map.

blocks, loaded onto camels, and sent throughout the region. A good salt loader knew how to put two or three blocks of salt weighing 40 to 50 pounds per block on a camel.

The camels carried the salt to places such as Ouagadougou, Djenne, Gao, and Kumbi. These were ancient cities, some dating back as far as 1000 B.C.E. A lively salt trade had been going on in these cities for years. They often traded gold for salt. Situated in the low savanna region of the continent, an area of broad, grassy meadows and sparse forests, these cities were easily reached by caravans of camel.

Some places in the salt trade could be reached by long cargo boats on the Niger River. If salt had to be transported further south into the forest region, then long human "trains" of men would carry the salt.

Although Ghana would last until the middle of the 13th century, it simply could not unite the different regions and keep control. Ghana's decline was rooted in overreaching its ability to govern its vast territory. Uprisings on the fringes of the Ghanaian Empire created problems within the central government that were never solved. Ghana's empire began to crumble slowly.

As the Ghana Empire began to weaken, the people began to lose confidence in their traditions, the country was weakened internally and, eventually, defeated easily by stronger neighbors.

CENTER YOUR THINKING

1. Explain how Ghana kept total control over all the natural resources of western Africa. How did taxation benefit the Ghanaian empire?

2. The king of Ghana owned all the gold nuggets. Explain why this might have been a good idea.

3. **CRITICAL THINKING:** Tell three reasons why salt was a precious commodity. Why do you think the Ghanaians were so secretive about the origin of the salt?

CHAPTER

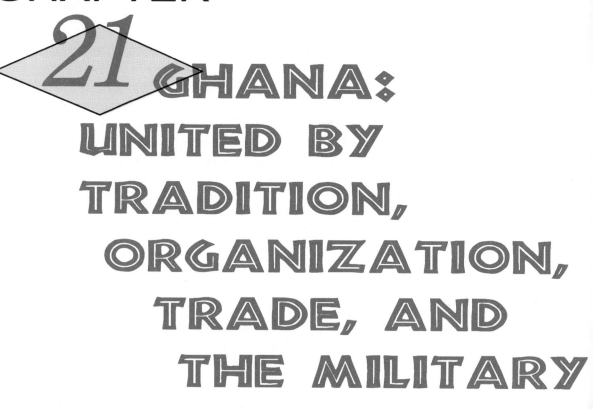

21 GHANA: UNITED BY TRADITION, ORGANIZATION, TRADE, AND THE MILITARY

VOCABULARY
principle   priority
commerce

CENTER YOUR VOCABULARY
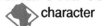 character

STRENGTH THROUGH TRADITION

One reason that Ghana became a great civilization was that it had strong cultural patterns, principles, and traditions that united all the people. Even before reaching its height as a military and economic power in the 7th century C.E., Ghana held fast to its principles of cultural integrity. These principles included respect for the king as the embodiment of the life of the nation.

The kingdom of Ghana had three national priorities. They were organization, control of commerce and trade, and a strong military force. These priorities served the kingdom well and, along with its strong culture, held Ghana together and helped it become a major power.

The Ghanaian kings built a powerful political organization on top of the strong traditional culture of the people. The kings built this organization through priests, teachers, governors, and lesser kings and nobles who ruled over small kingdoms. Each section of the country was ruled by a king or noble serving as governor. The governor was directly responsible to the king. Each governor had ministers who reported to him or her.

The country of Ghana controlled commerce, or trading, with people both north and south of the Ghana Empire. The gold, salt, ebony, and diamonds under the control of the Ghanaian Empire were sources of great wealth. Ghanaians traded these for other goods.

With so much wealth, the kingdom of Ghana needed a strong army. The Ghanaian Empire built a powerful military force. Ghana would eventually be defeated but not for at least four hundred years. The historian, Al-Zubri, wrote that the people of Ghana were so strong because their army fought with iron swords and lances, while other armies fought with ebony sticks.

Ghana's military controlled the gold fields of Bambuk to the south and west of Kumbi Saleh, the capital city. In addition, Ghana controlled the valuable trade routes to and from Audoghast, the southern frontier of Morocco.

While Ghana was preoccupied with controlling its large empire and pushing its borders farther south, the Almoravids formed a powerful and threatening army in the north around the city of Audoghast.

The Almoravids were a group with rigid Islamic religious beliefs and ideals. Under the leader Yaya ibn Umar, the Almoravids recaptured the city of Audoghast in 1055 C.E. in a bitter war with Ghana. After Yaya ibn Umar's victory, Abu Bakr reigned in the Audoghast region from 1056 to 1087 C.E.

Another battle between the Almoravids and Ghana around 1076 C.E. was the beginning of the end of Ghana as it had existed in greatness. Ghana lost this decisive battle and did not recover.

Ghana was forced to convert to Islam by the zealous Almoravids. Now Ghana had to submit to the influence of the Muslim preachers. Other people of the Ghanaian Empire, the Sosso and the Malinke, began to look for ways to express their own national characters. Sumanguru, a king of the southern Soninke, broke away from the central leadership of Ghana and defeated the capital city in 1204 C.E. He established his own rule over what was left of Ghana.

CENTER YOUR THINKING

1. What was the "common thread" that held Ghana together and made it a great civilization? What were ancient Ghana's three national priorities?

2. Compare ancient Ghana's political structure with that of the United States today. How are they alike? How are they different? Explain your answer.

3. CRITICAL THINKING: Review the events that led to the downfall and demise of the kingdom of ancient Ghana. Explain how they spelled doom for Ghana.

CHAPTER 22
RELIGION AND TRADE IN GHANA

VOCABULARY
worship   assembly

CENTER YOUR VOCABULARY

ancestor
lifestyle

INTENSELY PERSONAL RELIGION

The traditional religion of the people of Ghana was based upon a great ancestor, who was responsible for establishing the society in an earlier period. Sacred places and holy sites held the image of the ancestor god as a statue. Some sites had oracles, or places where the god spoke, attended by priests or priestesses.

The king was the most perfect representative of the god. People honored the king as the direct presence of the god on earth.

There were no written scriptures like the Bible or the Koran. The religion of Ghana was passed down from one generation to the next. Each family had one person who learned the traditions, rituals, and history. That person was important because he or she was responsible for passing all the religious information and beliefs down to others in the family.

The religion of Ghana was intensely personal and very family oriented. There were no great houses, temples, or churches where all the people gathered to worship. There was no need. Each family had a person who was in charge of the religion. And the people gathered when the king called them together at his palace.

A symbol of origin and fertility from Mali called a *chi-wara*
▼

A king's assembly was an extremely important event. At the king's assemblies, he represented the god on earth. The king and perhaps the chief minister would speak. The people would be asked to comment on the ideas just presented to them. In the end, however, the king, as god, gave the final word.

ISLAM COMES TO GHANA

Traders from the north brought their beliefs in a different religion to Ghana — the religion of Islam. This religion was new. Many Ghanaians began to follow Islam after the king received gifts from the traders and let them stay in the kingdom.

The religion of *Islam,* literally "submission to Allah," was started by the prophet Mohammed in Arabia in 622 C.E. The believer, called a Muslim, was to surrender all to the will of Allah, the Almighty God. Mohammed was a committed teacher and a great warrior, and he spread Islam from Mecca to Medina in Arabia and then into Africa. When he was disliked and abused by the people of Mecca, Mohammed left for the city of Medina, where his converts grew in number until he was able to return to Mecca and take over the city.

The African, Bilal, became Mohammed's close friend and one of the most famous Muslims because of the beauty and power of his voice in calling Muslim believers to prayer. Bilal and Abu Bakr, Mohammed's uncle from Arabia, were two of the key people in the spread of the religion in its early days.

Among the main principles, or the five pillars, of the religion of Islam are these:

The believer must confess that there is no god but God, and Mohammed is his prophet.

The believer must pray five times a day.

The believer must give charity, *zakat,* to the poor.

The believer must fast during the month of Ramadan.

The believer must make a pilgrimage, or sacred journey, called the *hajj,* to Mecca.

Neither the king of Ghana nor the people could appreciate all of the attitudes and behaviors of the Islamic newcomers. These newcomers were traders, but they also were preachers of Islam. They wanted to change the way the people of Ghana dressed, the language they spoke, their lifestyle, and the god they respected and worshiped. It seemed that these newcomers traded in both goods and religion.

Entering the empire of Ghana in the 9th century, the Muslim clerics, or religious teachers, became regular visitors to the great cities of the country. They set up trade and became religious teachers of the local population.

The Muslim clerics also used the Koran, the sacred book of Islam, as an instrument in their attempt to convert the local people to the Islamic religion.

Since the people of Ghana had maintained their religion only through the memory of their priests, the presence of a written holy book, the Koran, was as useful among the Africans as the Bible, another holy book, would be in other parts of the continent.

Soon Arab traders from both Arabia and the East would be found in almost every major city of the Ghanaian Empire. They would know more about the extent of the empire than many Ghana officials because their trade had taken them to all four corners of the empire. Large cities often had several areas where the Arabs were allowed to stay. In most cases, they were not allowed to stay inside the same areas where the citizens of the empire stayed. They were literally treated as outsiders, often having to stay 6 to 8 kilometers (4 to 5 miles) outside of the main cities.

At first, the older cities of Ghana presented the greatest opposition to Islam. But when these cities fell to the religion of Islam, it was just a matter of time before the rest of the empire would submit to the new religion. Some kings publicly accepted the religion for trade and political purposes, but privately held to their own religious traditions.

North of the city of Bamako in present day Mali, there are extensive stone remains of an ancient city. In ancient times, this area was part of Ghana. Discoveries of the ancient cities of Ghana are to be expected. Some of the buildings discovered north of Bamako suggest that the city was very large. There could have been more than thirty thousand people in the ancient town. Many historians think that it was the site of the great royal city of Ghana.

Such a central city, with so many fine buildings, must have been the site of visits from foreign dignitaries. Such dignitaries would have come from Africa as well as other parts of the ancient world. The king who controlled the Ghanaian Empire would have been the equal of any king in the world in the year 950 C.E.

Tunkamenin, one of the great kings of Ghana, had an army of more than 250,000 soldiers. It included infantry and cavalry. At the height of its strength in the 10th century C.E., the army of Ghana could defeat any army in Africa and perhaps in the world.

Trained in the art of warfare on the savanna fields and the *sahel,* the Ghanaian soldiers, according to observers, were prepared to defend their trade routes with fierce military might. However, it would only be a matter of time before their superiority was challenged.

CENTER YOUR THINKING

1. Explain at least two major ideas or beliefs in the religion of ancient Ghana.

2. What role did religion play in changing the course of history for ancient Ghana? Explain your answer.

3. Visit the library and research the city of Bamako in ancient Ghana. How have scholars and archaeologists learned from the discoveries of this ancient city in present day Mali?

CHAPTER

23 THE END OF THE GREAT EMPIRE OF GHANA

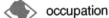
THE BERBER CHALLENGE

The power of the army of Ghana did not last. Challenged by the growing military prowess of the Berber ethnic groups to the north and west of the capital city, Kumbi, the Ghanaian Empire spent considerable time and military energy putting down local rebellions among the Berber. Unable to cope with all of the Berber uprisings or the newly formed Berber religious movement, the Almoravids, Ghana found itself constantly at war with the northerners.

As the army of Ghana weakened, it could not defend itself from the combined forces of the religiously inspired Almoravid soldiers and a collection of former vassal states. A *vassal state* is a nation that owes its protection to another nation. A major uprising was created by the two groups. The smaller and weaker nations surrounding Ghana joined forces with the Almoravids to confront the Empire of Ghana.

In 1054 C.E., the Almoravids captured the Ghanaian city of Audoghast. This was a major defeat for Ghana. Audoghast was the center of the salt trade. Now the chief city for the salt trade was in the hands of the Almoravids. Ghana could no longer control the terms of trade. This was a bad sign for the kingdom of Ghana.

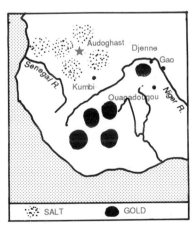

▲ In 1054 C.E., the Almoravids captured Audoghast, and the salt trade was in their control.

The Almoravids were not satisfied with stopping their conquest at Audoghast, the salt capital. They wanted to own the gold centers, too. Many more battles ensued between the two major forces in West Africa. By 1076 C.E., the Almoravids were at the gates of the great city of Kumbi. They overran the army of Ghana and sacked the entire city. They looted its libraries, raided its gold deposits, and plundered the wealth of the citizens.

Now it was the people of Ghana who had to pay tribute and taxes to another African power. This was a new experience for the Ghanaian empire. For more than a thousand years, it had been supreme.

The people of Ghana took their loss and the occupation of their country by the Almoravids very hard. The Almoravids not only brought Islam with them, they forced the people of Ghana to accept the new religion. Islamic mosques were built throughout the land. The names of the Ghanaian people were changed to Arabic names. The Almoravid occupation of the land lasted for 50 years.

By the time the Soninke, a people who belonged to the Ghanaian empire, overthrew the Almoravids in 1087 C.E., new nations had arisen around the Ghanaian territory. Older vassal states had gained strength and independence. One new kingdom was the small Malinke kingdom of Mali.

According to traditional tales or oral historians, Sumanguru, a king of Ghana, defeated the Malinke king of Mali in 1203 C.E. and added the area to his own land and rule. After Sumanguru had killed the Malinke king, he systematically killed all of the king's heirs — all, that is, except one.

The one heir of the king of Mali who was not killed was a toddler whose legs were physically handicapped. He was known as Sundiata Keita. He grew up to become the first king of the great empire of Mali and the most honored leader in West African history. Sundiata defeated the armies of Ghana and made his people, the Malinke, the core of the Mali Empire, the single most dominant power in West Africa. Sumanguru's people, the Sosso, who had ruled as the elite of Ghana, became vassals to the new, emergent Mali kingdom.

CENTER YOUR THINKING

1. Explain how the Almoravid people were able to dominate the ancient empire of Ghana.

2. Analyze and explain the importance of trade for the Almoravid people.

3. **CRITICAL THINKING:** What impact do you feel that religion and military conquests had on the lives of ancient Africans through the years? Create a timeline to put your feelings into a sequence. Can you identify any famous African Americans who have accepted Islam? Add them to your timeline.

UNIT REVIEW

The greatness of the empire of Ghana is well documented by the ancient historian, Al-Bakri, in a book describing his travels to Ghana in 1968 C.E. (p. 95) He marvels, as do modern scholars today, at Ghana's greatness, resulting from setting clear national priorities: organization, control of trade and commerce, and a strong military force. (p.100)

Ghana controlled inflation in its economy so that no one group could far exceed another in setting prices and becoming excessively wealthy. This gave the people a great sense of security and is a model for today. The ancient rulers were well aware that the economic situation of people was one key to keeping them satisfied and peaceful. (p. 98)

Religion in Ghana was intensely personal, rather than dictated by a leader. There was no written religious book, but each family had one person whose duty it was to keep an oral history of the religion and their beliefs. This made Ghana a strongly united nation in terms of national traditions that were deeply felt and a strong sense of family. (p. 103)

PERSONAL WITNESSING

REFLECTION

Most religions and systems of belief have a set of basic beliefs. Think about what you believe. Could you list for yourself the important beliefs that guide your life? Should anyone be forced to accept the beliefs of another? How can you share your beliefs with others without being forceful?

TESTIMONY

How do you think the Almoravids felt about capturing the wealth of Ghana? Write a poem or a rap, or create a performance to illustrate. Some poem starters follow to help you.

We're known as mighty warriors
across the burning sands.
Those who defy us will perish by our hands!

UNIT 6

"Culture serves as the facilitator of customs, values, and behavior. In Mali we find cultural riches for eternity."

— **Kariamu Welsh**

MALI: THE MAGNIFICENT EMPIRE

The most famous empire of West Africa was the kingdom of Mali. Throughout the ancient world, the name of Mali was identified with the glories of Africa.

CENTER YOURSELF

Sundiata, the great king of Mali, overcame tremendous obstacles and built the magnificent Empire of Mali. Do you know of someone who overcame tremendous physical, social, or economic odds to succeed? What kinds of challenges did that person have to conquer? How were the achievements and obstacles like Sundiata's? How were they different?

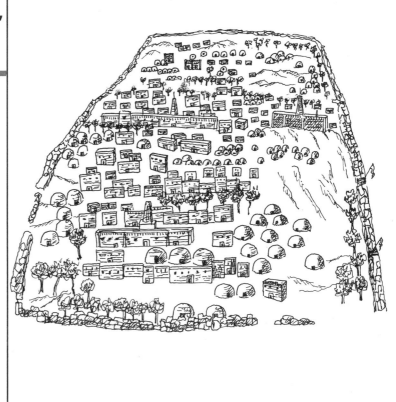

The city of Timbuktu was the greatest city in Africa and one of the greatest cities in the world in the 13th century C.E.

CHAPTER
24 SUNDIATA

SUNDIATA AND MALI OVERCOME OBSTACLES

Sundiata was one of the most important leaders in the history of Africa. He was intelligent, brave, and diplomatic. The birth of Sundiata occurred during a time when the people of the small country of Mali were at their lowest. Mali had suffered greatly at the hands of its enemies.

Mali existed as an independent kingdom from around the first century C.E. The ruling family was the Keita family. They produced the kings and queens of Mali for more than 13 centuries. In fact, the Keita legacy remains a source of pride for the people of West Africa.

Mali became famous and a player on the world stage in 1230 C.E. That was the year that Sundiata, the son of Nare Maghan I, ascended the throne of the kingdom of Kankaba. Sundiata's mother was Sogolon Kedju, the second wife of the king Nare Maghan. In Mali, the king usually had more than one wife at a time. Sogolon was a woman of great intelligence and a powerful personality. She cared for her son Sundiata with extreme patience since he had been born with one leg shorter than the other. Sogolon watched her son to see that he developed a good sense of personal esteem.

The king's first wife, Sassouma, did not like Sogolon Kedju. Every time she could find something wrong with Sogolon, she would criticize her before the king. The fact that Sogolon's son had one short leg made Sassouma think of herself as superior. However, Sassouma would quickly learn that greatness had nothing to do with a person's legs.

Sundiata was an outstanding boy. He worked every day to overcome his physical difficulties. He strengthened his legs with exercise. He ran in the savanna with the other boys. He practiced his speaking skills to the small sand dunes outside of his village. Sundiata wanted to master diplomacy, the art of saying the right thing at the right time in order to get people to come to agreement. He was a very studious young man who paid attention to the way people talked, behaved, and related to each other.

KING SUNDIATA AND MALI RISE TO GREATNESS

Sundiata became a charismatic and great leader at a young age. He took over his father's throne from his half brother who had mishandled it. Sundiata was about 20 years old when he was made king in 1230 C.E.

He soon began to prepare Mali to rid itself of the cruel king of Ghana, Sumanguru. At that time, no king was more feared than Sumanguru. He had led his armies against all the states that had challenged his power. Mali had been one of his victims. Sumanguru had tried to kill off all the heirs of Nare Maghan, king of Mali. But Sumanguru had not killed Sundiata in order to demonstrate pity on the young boy with one leg shorter than the other. This proved to be a tragic mistake for Sumanguru because Sundiata would later meet him at the battle of Kirina.

Legend has it that, as Sundiata's army advanced to meet Sumanguru's army, Sumanguru, the Ghanaian king, thought he was seeing a stone mountain advancing toward him. But when Sundiata saw Sumanguru's army, he thought it was only a cloud! The two columns of soldiers locked in fierce battle behind their kings.

Sundiata told one of his generals, Sangara Danguinia Konnte, to go to the front of the column armed with a spear while grasping the spur, or leg, of a white cock, or rooster. He told Sangara to throw the spear at Sumanguru.

As Sangara threw the spear at Sumanguru, he shouted, "This is the spear of he who knows the ancient secrets." Sumanguru was killed on the spot. When his body was buried, all his gold bracelets, amulets, and chains were buried with him. Legend has it that at Kirina, one can see a baobab tree that grew on the exact spot where Sumanguru died.

The battle of Kirina, one of the great and decisive battles in African history, was fought in 1240 C.E. between the armies of Sumanguru and Sundiata. Spurred on by the praise singer Balla Fasseke Kuyate, who kept saying to Sundiata, "You Maghan, you are Mali," Sundiata emerged victorious over the cruel Sumanguru. With this victory, Sundiata reunited the remnants of Mali under his authority and laid the foundation for a new empire.

Sundiata was not only respected by the people of Mali as a military leader who succeeded in defeating Mali's enemies, but also as a diplomat who made peace with his neighbors and won allies for the empire. There had never been a king like Sundiata in Mali. He enlarged the kingdom. At the same time, he paid close attention to those areas that did not support him completely. He constantly watched for new enemies and threats.

As a military strategist, Sundiata put the control of his armies under several valiant generals. Although he participated in battles, often leading the attacks, he was not the only military leader. With an organized military, Sundiata

The Empire of Mali

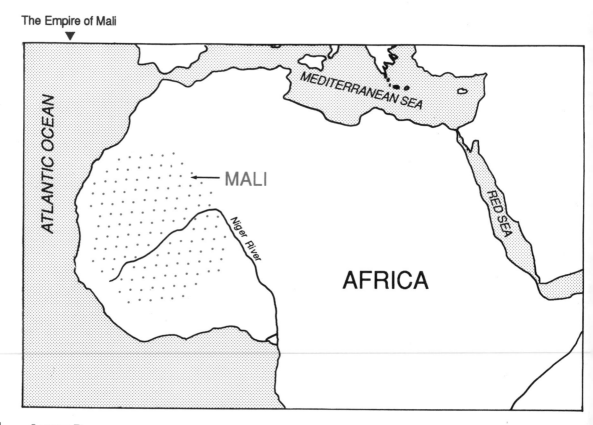

could rely upon his generals to carry out their duties according to his orders. This gave him a unique opportunity to share responsibility for governance of the empire.

The kingdom of Mali, larger than Europe, stretched for more than 2,420 kilometers (1,500 miles) east to west. No one person could have managed to oversee such a huge empire without the support and aid of others. Sundiata's type of management, sharing his authority and responsibility, was a new approach to government in West Africa.

Sundiata died in 1255 C.E. At his death, Mali was the richest state in all of West Africa. No state in Europe was better organized or more committed to protecting its citizens than Mali. No state in Africa had ruled more territory and controlled more wealth. The foundation of an even greater empire had been laid and Mali, after Sundiata, would establish itself in history as a civilization unparalleled in West Africa.

CENTER YOUR THINKING

1. What is the name of the most famous empire of West Africa? Tell about the empire, its size, the ruling family, and its communities.

2. How did Sundiata deal with his physical problems? How did he discipline himself to become such a strong leader? Tell how the battle of Kirina established the greatness of both the Empire of Mali and King Sundiata.

3. CRITICAL THINKING: Do you think that Sundiata's childhood physical problems helped to make him a successful leader? Why or why not? Explain your answer.

CHAPTER 25

MALI AFTER SUNDIATA

VOCABULARY

hierarchical   *cadi*
patriarchal   generosity

CENTER YOUR VOCABULARY

 dignity

MANSA MUSA RESTORES MALI'S GREATNESS

None of the new kings who succeeded Sundiata had his charisma, personal power, or diplomatic and leadership skills. Instead of working hard as rulers, the immediate successors to the great king spent their time in court intrigues and trying to consolidate their own power.

Then the grand nephew of Sundiata, Mansa Musa, came to power at a time when it seemed that the great kingdom of Mali was without direction. Mansa Musa ruled between 1307 C.E. and 1332 C.E.

It is reported during this period in 1305 C.E. that Abubakari, a relative of Mansa Musa, ordered 100 fishing vessels to be sent

An artist's drawing of
King Mansa Musa ▶

across the ocean. The historian Al-Omari, writing in his book, *Masalik Absad Masalik,* says that the emperor told him the following.

> *"The monarch who preceded me would not believe that it was impossible to discover the limits of the neighboring sea. He wished to know. He persisted in his plan. He caused the equipping of two hundred ships and filled them with men, and other another such number that were filled with gold, water and food for two years. He said to the commanders: Do not return until you have reached the end of the ocean, or when you have exhausted your food and water.*
>
> *"They went away and their absence was long: none came back, and their absence continued. Then a single ship returned. We asked the captain of their adventures and their news. He replied: Sultan, we sailed on, but as each of them came to that place they did not come back nor did they reappear; and I do not know what became of them. As for me, I turned where I was and did not enter the current."*

Mansa Musa rebuilt the capital city. He added new territories that paid taxes to Mali. Mansa Musa gained greater control over more of the vast salt mines in the south, extending the empire into Guinea in the south and the Mossi country in the west.

Mansa Musa organized his entire kingdom in a hierarchical way. Governors, district officers, and village chiefs all submitted to the will of the paramount king, Mansa Musa. More than 200,000 soldiers served in the army of Mali. But the large army was manageable because it was hierarchical, organized with certain ranks in charge of lower ranks. This type of military structure was to be repeated among the Yoruba, Asante, Baule, and other nations.

The provinces were headed by governors who could be appointed or dismissed by the emperor himself. His system of justice was structured around a supreme judge, the *cadi*, who, along with a council of wise men and elders, handed down their decisions and dispensed justice from the capital city of Niani. Increasingly, Mali became a patriarchal society unlike earlier West African governments.

Mansa Musa is best remembered for his 1324 C.E. pilgrimage, or holy trip, to Mecca in Arabia. On the way to Mecca, he caused inflation in Egypt, hurting the Egyptian economy. This was because of the large amount of gold spent by his entourage as they traveled through Egypt. Gold was so freely spent by Mansa Musa and members of his party that the people of Egypt and Arabia were amazed. The king of Mali owned and controlled the rich gold mines in the south of his country. His presence in Egypt and Arabia with so much gold must have created quite a stir.

The emperor took with him more than 500 servants, each carrying a gold bar weighing more than a pound. But gold was not the only valuable taken on the trip. Other caravans carried food and water. All in all, about a thousand people, many on camels, went with Mansa Musa, crossing the desert, entering Egypt, and finally traveling on to Mecca in the company of the greatest king of West Africa at the time. As a devout Muslim, Mansa Musa, showed his generosity by bestowing many gifts on the local people. The wealth of Mansa Musa was largely based on his gold holdings. He might be referred to as "the Golden Emperor."

This Golden Emperor controlled much of the gold of the Senegal and Niger river valleys. He taxed the vassal states that were under him. He taxed the salt from Teghaza and the copper from Diara. His influence and wealth grew with the opening of each new gold field, each new salt mine, and each trade route across the desert.

Mansa Musa also encouraged education. Universities were set up at Djenne, Gao, and Timbuktu. Because of his international interest, Mansa Musa encouraged scholars from the north to come to his universities. He also sent Malian scholars to other universities.

Mansa Musa, like many kings, built new, important buildings that demonstrated his power. His most important building projects were the mosques set up in all the big cities of the empire. The architect, Es-Saleh, whom he had commissioned to build several mosques and monuments, was

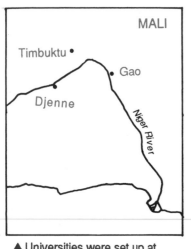

▲ Universities were set up at Djenne, Gao, and Timbuktu.

impressed with the king's generosity. He had been brought from Egypt to Mali as a royal architect. Since Es-Saleh was handsomely rewarded for his services, he remained the chief architect for many years.

Mansa Musa ruled the Empire of Mali as the most powerful and respected leader of the Africa of his day. He kept his power by listening to others, examining their goals and aims, and giving them freedom to discuss their needs. Although Mansa Musa was Islamic, he did not force all the people in Mali to follow his religion. The Wangara mining group chose not to become Islamic. Mansa Musa, recognizing the power of the people, said that they would not be forced to convert to Islam.

Mansa Musa gave a new dignity to the African people by focusing on their needs. Perhaps this is a lesson for us today. Taking care of so large a kingdom is almost impossible unless there are many trustworthy people to share the power and responsibility.

CULTURE AND THE ARTS IN MALI

Malians were silversmiths, goldsmiths, coppersmiths, bronze workers, weavers, iron smelters, tanners, and dyers. They performed dances and ceremonies in honor of their ancestors. These dances were a way to teach their children respect and generosity. Under the enlightened reign of the great Mansa Musa, the arts flourished as the kingdom of Mali prospered.

The wealth of the Malian Empire was used to create art. The kingdom of Mali had enormous wealth in gold, copper, iron, salt, and subsistence crops. Big cities of commerce included Niani, Ualata, Timbuktu, Gao, Djenne, and Kankan.

Malian scholars and authors used the Arabic script when they wrote histories, biographies, and religious texts. Using the Arabic script for Africans during the Mali Empire is comparable to us using Phoenician alphabet to write English or French. Thus, the Africans whose language may have been Yoruba or Mande could use the Arabic script to record their histories.

Many African and Arab writers wrote about the Mali Empire. Among the African writers who wrote informatively

This intricate bronze anklet is from Mali.
▼

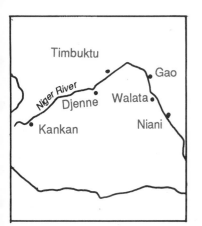

▲ Mali's major cities of commerce

Timbuktu
Niger River
Djenne
Kankan
Gao
Walata
Niani

about Mali was Ibn Battuta. He spent a year in the capital of Mali and wrote:

> "The Malians possessed some admirable qualities. They are seldom unjust and have a greater abhorrence of injustice than any other people.
>
> "The Sultan shows no mercy to anyone who is guilty of the least act of malice. There is complete security in their country. Neither traveler nor inhabitant in it has to fear robbers or men of violence. They do not confiscate the property of any Arab who dies in their country, even if it were of great wealth. On the contrary they give it into the charge of some trustworthy person among the Arabs until the rightful heir takes possession of it. They are careful to observe the hours of prayer and assiduous in attending them in congregations and take their children, also."

Ibn Battuta had come from Morocco in the north and found that the people of the empire had a great sense of justice. They received foreigners with open arms and did not attack either them or their property.

Many foreigners journeyed to Mali for adventure and trade. But, as we can see, few visitors were as vigilant in recording what they saw as the African traveler, Ibn Battuta. He went to Mali in 1352 C.E.

Ibn Battuta traveled from Sijilmasa to Teghaza to Walata. When he arrived in Walata, he was shocked to see the high social status accorded to women. He went from Walata to Niane and stayed in the Mali Empire many months, traveling and learning before he returned to Fez.

Among his observations about the Mali Empire are these:

The emperor wears a red velvety tunic.

The emperor wears a golden skullcap.

The emperor is preceded by musicians.

A cord of the bow is plucked to confirm a speaker's words.

Battuta also said that the people of the Mali Empire had the following qualities:

> a small number of acts of injustice because the people are, of all peoples, those who most abhor (hate) injustice,

> complete and general safety throughout the land,

> The people do not confiscate the goods of the Arabs.

> The people are very religious and make their prayers punctually.

> They wear white garments on Friday.

> They commit the Koran (the holy book of Islam) to memory.

It is obvious that the culture of the Mali Empire was strongly reliant upon both the religion of Islam and the traditional African culture. It was, in large part, the traditional African society that impressed Ibn Battuta.

CENTER YOUR THINKING

1. What happened to the kingdom of Mali immediately after Sundiata's death? Why did this happen?

2. Analyze and explain what happened to make Mali begin to become a great empire again. Give at least three causes that contributed to this change. How did trading routes help to change the downward trend for Mali?

3. CRITICAL THINKING: What do you think we should learn from Mansa Musa's leadership for today's world? Explain your answer.

UNIT REVIEW

King Sundiata of Mali was one of the most important leaders in the history of all of Africa. He revived the greatness of the ancient African empire. (p.112)

The scholars and authors of Mali wrote using the Arabic script, giving a common script for writing to the different African countries and languages. (p.119)

Mansa Musa was not only a powerful but also a highly respected ruler. He gave the people great freedom, listening to them and their needs before making decisions. Although he was Islamic, he did not force his religion on the African people. (p. 119)

PERSONAL WITNESSING

REFLECTION

Reflect on the thoughts and concerns that Mansa Musa might have had on his *hajj,* or religious pilgrimage, to Mecca in 1324 C.E. How would you feel if you had been Mansa Musa? What would you worry about and prepare for, with your large caravan? What would be your personal concerns and spiritual thoughts? What might you hope to gain as a person from your trip to a holy place?

TESTIMONY

Think about one or more people who have been role models or key people in making you who you are today and in building your self-esteem. Make some notes on how each person has helped you and how you wish to help others as a result. Share with the class how you wish to help others in serving as a role model because of your experiences. You do not have to share your personal experiences or name the people, but, instead, share what you wish to do to help others because of your experiences. In sharing, you should respect the feelings of everyone in the class.

"There are many judges, doctors, and clerics here, all receiving good salaries from King Askia Mohammed of Songhay. There is a great demand for books, and more profit is made from the trade in books than from any other line of business."

— Leo Africanus

SONGHAY: LAND OF ROYALTY

Songhay was the last of the great kingdoms of West Africa. After its decline, there was general instability throughout all of Africa.

CENTER YOURSELF

The famous African teacher, Ahmed Baba, was a legendary scholar at the University of Sankore during the glory of the Songhay Empire. Imagine that you were one of his students when he was arrested and taken away in chains by the Moroccan army. How would you feel? What would you do to try to continue his African path of knowledge and his training of others?

Sunni Ali Ber was the greatest of the Songhay rulers, building the Songhay Empire to be the most powerful force in West Arica.

CHAPTER

26 THE RULE OF SUNNI ALI BER

VOCABULARY
placate   annex
siege

CENTER YOUR VOCABULARY

dynasty
reformer

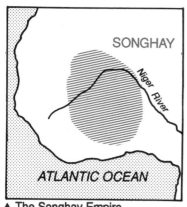
▲ The Songhay Empire

Sunni Ali Ber ▼

INNOVATION AND TRADITION

The small kingdom of Gao was a vassal state of the Malian Empire during the reign of the Golden Emperor, Mansa Musa. Gao belonged to Mansa Musa and was ruled by him.

The kingdom of Gao had been founded by a wise king, Dia Assibia. He had established a dynasty that ruled for sixteen generations. The last descendant of Dia Assibia was Sunni Ali Ber, or Sovereign Ali the Great, as he was also called.

The religion of Islam sweeping across Africa from the east to the west during the 7th through 14th centuries C.E. left strong cultural marks on many African people. Islam accepts Allah as God, and Mohammed as his prophet. Mohammed lived in Arabia in the 7th century C.E.

Sunni Ali Ber knew he had to unite his empire, including the Islamic people and those who kept African beliefs. Sunni Ali Ber went so far as to take an Islamic name in his attempt to placate Africans who had become followers of Islam. However, Sunni Ali Ber resisted letting Islam or any other religion destroy traditional religions of Africa.

Sunni Ali Ber was a brilliant thinker, a good planner, and a fearless conqueror. He came to power in the year 1464 C.E. He regained Timbuktu, the ancient city, from the rule of the Tuareg people. Once he had expelled the Tuaregs from the city, he turned his attention to enlarging his kingdom.

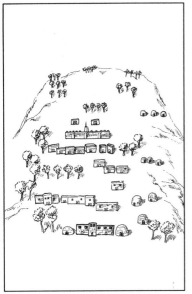

▲ This drawing of Djenne probably does not compare with the beauty of the ancient city.

Sunni Ali Ber annexed, or took over, all of the smaller states that had sworn allegiance to the Mali Empire. As he had regained Timbuktu, Sunni Ali Ber also took the great city of Djenne. It is said that the Mali had tried to defeat Djenne 99 times but were rebuffed each time.

Djenne was a difficult victory for Sunni Ali Ber. He had to lay siege to the city, extending his attacks for an extremely long time, trying to wear down the people of Djenne. The siege lasted for an incredible seven years, seven months, and seven days. Djenne finally fell in 1473 C.E.

In 1906, the historian, Lady Lugard, wrote in her book, *A Tropical Dependency,* about the victory:

"At the end of the siege, the town yielded by honorable capitulation. No injury of any kind was done to its inhabitants, and the seven days which are added to the period of the siege were consumed, it is said, by festivities on the occasion of the marriage of Sunni Ali with the widow of the ruler of the town who had died during the siege."

Djenne was one of the most beautiful, thriving cities in the Songhay Empire. It was a rich trading center, bustling with activity. Beautiful hills and valleys surrounded Djenne, making the setting a scenic one. The designs of the houses and public buildings were classic and noble in appearance.

Djenne was also the home of an advanced culture. A great university rivaling the famous one in Timbuktu was located in Djenne. The Djenne university was a center of medical education. Doctors at the university were even removing cataracts from the human eye at Djenne's medical school. In 1485, thousands of people worked in Djenne at the university, in the schools, in the trades, and in commerce and business. Djenne became, alongside Gao, Timbuktu, and other towns, the pride of Songhay.

Sunni Ali Ber's strategy was to secure the peace throughout the entire Sudanese region. Under the reign of Sunni Ali Ber, the Songhay kingdom became the largest of the Sudanese empires with a fleet of boats on the Niger River. His peace-keeping plan was successful largely because Sunni Ali Ber made sure that all his actions were aimed at keeping peace. Any enemies of Songhay were dealt with swiftly and effectively.

One reason that Sunni Ali Ber had a peace-keeping strategy was that he wanted to reestablish the presence of African culture in religion, education, and traditions throughout the empire. He was a reformer. He cleaned out the religious leaders in the institutions of learning and replaced them with intellectuals who understood the African traditions of the people.

By the time of his death in 1492 C.E., Sunni Ali Ber was the most powerful leader in all of Africa and one of the most important leaders in the world. Travelers from other parts of Africa and Europe reported that Sunni Ali Ber was the greatest leader in Africa. The Europeans referred to him as Sunni Heli, King of Timbuktu. They said that his empire extended to the coast of the Atlantic Ocean.

The Death of Sunni Ali Ber

Sunni Ali Ber left a highly organized and efficient government. His son, Bakori Da'as, came to power after him in 1492 C.E. His son, a Muslim like his father but with even less religious conviction than Sunni Ali Ber, was just as committed to preserving the traditional values of the people.

In less than ten months, the Muslims organized a revolution against Bakori Da'as because he sought to continue his father's assault on the foreign influences in Songhay.

Bakori Da'as was soon overthrown by Mamoudou Toure, General-in-Chief of the army of Gao, a devout Muslim. General Toure was crowned emperor of Songhay under the name of Askia Mohammed in 1493 C.E. As Askia Mohammed, he ruled until 1529 C.E.

The Important Kings of Songhay

Sunni Ali Ber ruled from 1464 C.E. to 1492 C.E.

Askia Mohammed ruled from 1493 C.E. to 1529 C.E.

Daoud Mohammed ruled from 1549 C.E. to 1582 C.E.

1. Why was Sunni Ali Ber called "Sovereign Ali the Great?" Why was Djenne a key victory for him?

2. What was Sunni Ali Ber's ultimate goal for Africa during his reign? How did his strategy of dealing swiftly with any influences or cultures that opposed his goal work against him and his son, Bakori Da'as?

3. **CRITICAL THINKING:** What was the role of religion during the reigns of Sunni Ali Ber and his son? How do you think that religion played a role in the overthrow of Bakori Da'as by Gao?

CHAPTER

27 ASKIA MOHAMMED REBUILDS THE EMPIRE

▲ A drawing of what Askia
Mohammed may have
looked like

ASKIA MOHAMMED REBUILDS A STRONG DECENTRALIZED GOVERNMENT, 1493 C.E. TO 1529 C.E

Askia Mohammed, like the Songhay leaders just before him, was a valiant and courageous conqueror. From the start of his reign, Askia Mohammed set out to rebuild Sunni Ali Ber's great empire. He took it upon himself to add to the kingdom's territory, power, and efficient organization. With the help of a group of outstanding administrators, Askia Mohammed could successfully decentralize the government, handing down power to his close advisors as governors of the provinces.

Perhaps Askia Mohammed decentralized his government to remove the possibility that any one of his advisors could become powerful enough to overthrow him. However, it seems more likely that the new emperor simply wanted to get more accurate information about what was happening in the outlying regions of his empire. The far regions would have been hard for the emperor to control from his central location. With more trusted governors to watch these far regions closely, on-site, Askia Mohammed could ascertain more about what was really going on there.

EMPEROR ASKIA MOHAMMED KEEPS TIGHT CONTROL

Askia Mohammed was able to control the movement of the nomadic Tuareg people, who did not settle but moved from place to place to find water for their animals. As nomads traveling between oases, places where they found water and fruit, the Tuaregs were experts in their knowledge of the desert. In the past, they had attacked the capitals of Mali and Songhay, often destroying the cities. Emperor Mohammed used his army to keep the Tuaregs on the outskirts of the cities. Askia Mohammed built more caravan roads across the vast Sahara desert region. In improving the roads, Mohammed made travel safe for traders as well as the military. This helped to stimulate trade.

Emperor Askia Mohammed did not shy away from military adventures against the neighboring states. In 1505 C.E., he sent an expedition against the Mossi states located to the east of Songhay. He not only succeeded in subduing them, he also brought some of their children to his capital to be raised as Muslims.

In 1513 C.E., the armed forces of Songhay entered the Hausa states to the southeast of Mossi and defeated most of the kingdoms along the Niger River as far as Lake Chad. Only the Kano state was not defeated. However, after a long siege, the king of Kano sued for peace. Askia Mohammed let the Kano king keep his throne but, of course, for a price. The Kano king had to pay an annual tribute of gold to Songhay.

Songhay, expansive and militarily strong, also attacked the nomadic Tauregs in the vicinity of Aïr during the year 1515 C.E. Songhay conquered the local people and settled Songhay people among them. This practice enabled the emperor to know of any impending attacks by the Tuaregs against Songhay.

Only the small kingdom of Kebbi, between the Hausa states and the Niger River, proved to be invincible and was never taken by Songhay. Protected by reinforced walls of mud and stone, the Kebbi warrior king, Kanta, kept his people independent. In 1517 C.E., Askia Mohammed stopped assaulting Kebbi.

Because he had a strong cabinet of ministers who reported directly to him, Askia Mohammed can be said to be the first modern ruler of the Sudanic region. He used his cabinet of expert people to assist him in organizing and ruling the country. These skilled government people were in charge of agriculture, water, forests, the navy, the army, the cavalry, finance, trade, and external affairs. The government appointed various other officers as needed for collecting taxes, controlling prices, regulating caravans, and deciding legal cases.

Our government's cabinet is very similar to that of African emperor Askia Mohammed's. ▼

PRESIDENT CLINTON'S CABINET	EMPEROR ASKIA MOHAMMED'S CABINET
Departments:	
State	External Affairs
Treasury	Finance
Defense	Navy
	Cavalry
Interior	Forests
Justice	Legal Affairs
Agriculture	Agriculture
Commerce	Trade
Transportation	Caravans
Labor	
Housing & Urban Development	
Energy	
Health & Human Services	
Veteran's Affairs	

1. Why did the author describe Askia Mohammed as a valiant and courageous conqueror? Give at least three adjectives to describe Askia Mohammed, and explain why you selected each one.

2. How did Askia Mohammed use his trusted governors to help him rule? What were some of their responsibilities? How did they help Askia Mohammed control the movements of the Tuareg people?

3. **CRITICAL THINKING:** Why was the small kingdom of Kebbi never conquered by Askia Mohammed? How do you think this made him feel?

CHAPTER

28 RELIGION, THE ARTS, AND CULTURE UNDER ASKIA MOHAMMED

VOCABULARY
motif   wane
model

CENTER YOUR VOCABULARY
pilgrimage

ISLAM, ART, AND CULTURE FLOURISH

The religion of Islam flourished under Emperor Askia Mohammed, as did the arts and African culture. Artisans used religious symbols on leather and jewelry. Architects built mosques that reflected Islamic motifs, or designs. Poets sang the praises of Islamic heroes. The Arabic script was widely used as a symbol of art. Since Islam did not encourage painting and sculpture, many traditional artists were unable to perform. However, Islam gave Africa an entirely different influence than the traditional religions.

Askia Mohammed, a good Muslim, went to Mecca in 1495 C.E. But his religious pilgrimage, though impressive, was less flamboyant than that of the Malian emperor, Mansa Musa, who made his pilgrimage about 200 years earlier.

Askia Mohammed, like Mansa Musa, did not make his pilgrimage alone. He was accompanied to Mecca, the Holy City of Islam, by an army of 1,000 infantry and a cavalry of 500 horsemen. According to the records of the trip, some 300,000 pieces of gold were budgeted for the journey. One third of the amount was used to cover the costs of travel. Another third was for gifts to the poor. The final third was used to buy supplies, goods, and lodging in Mecca.

When Askia Mohammed returned to Songhay from his pilgrimage to Mecca in 1495 C.E. he began to restore the influence of Islam that had waned under Sunni Ali Ber and the short reign of Bakori Da'as. Askia Mohammed became Islam's most vigorous proponent in West Africa. The universities were changed to reflect an Islamic model and way of thinking.

African Culture and Education Are Filtered Through Islam

Askia Mohammed himself practiced Islam as a devout and faithful believer. Sunni Ali Ber had tried to make the empire's education and religion more like classical Africa rather than just Islamic, for example, by changing the university structure and education at Timbuktu. Sunni Ali Ber had not emphasized any one religion but, instead, had emphasized the different African religions and ways of thinking.

The Koran is the holy book of Islam.

Askia Mohammed, however, instilled a stronger Islamic influence in education. He stopped the decline in Islamic education. The University of Sankore at Timbuktu was restored to its glory. It excelled in Islamic law, literature, rhetoric, logic, medicine, and mathematics. Under the reign of Sunni Ali Ber, the Islamic education had been discouraged. Clerics, or Islamic religious leaders, had been in disfavor, and local religious leaders had been elevated.

The great professor Ahmed Baba, last vice chancellor of the University of Sankore in the 16th century, was the principal scholar of this time. Professor Baba wrote more than 40 books in fields as diverse as astronomy, biography, and theology. His own library contained 1,600 volumes on various topics. He is credited with establishing a tradition of apprentice that is still widely practiced in West Africa. Students came to learn with him and often left after ten years. Supported by the emperor, Ahmed Baba became a legend in his time because of his intelligence, discipline, and scholarship.

The African love of knowledge, literature, and learning, although now filtered through the religion of Islam, never died. As it had been in the days of the early Egyptian kingdom, so it was in the days of Askia Mohammed. In fact, Leo Africanus, a historian of the 16th century, wrote about Timbuktu:

"There are many judges, doctors, and clerics here, all receiving good salaries from King Askia Mohammed of the state of Songhay. He pays great respect to men of learning. There is a great demand for books, and more profit is made from the trade in books than from any other line of business."

CENTER YOUR THINKING

1. Tell at least two ways that we know today that the arts and culture flourished under Askia Mohammed and Islam.

2. Why did Askia Mohammed make a journey to Mecca in 1495 C.E.? How was his journey like Mansa Musa's? How was it different? Give at least two similarities and two differences.

3. **CRITICAL THINKING:** How did Askia Mohammed's rule and philosophy for the African people differ from Sunni Ali Ber's? How do you think each ruler would have described what he wanted the African people to achieve?

CHAPTER 29

MOROCCO DOOMS THE SONGHAY EMPIRE

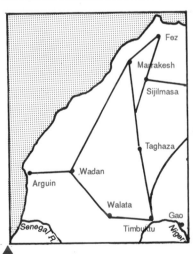

The trans-Saharan trade routes

ASKIA MOHAMMED'S DOWNFALL

Askia Mohammed became blind in 1529 C.E. He increasingly lost control over the far-flung parts of the empire. Challenges to his authority became regular and frequent.

Finally, Askia Mohammed was dethroned by his own sons. They turned out to be very weak rulers. When the great Askia Mohammed made his transition from life to death on March 2, 1538 C.E., he was 97 years old. The people of the Songhay Empire mourned his death. But they also lamented the fact that his sons, neither of whom had Askia Mohammed's strong character and integrity, were now in control of the government.

The sons were conniving and petty and did not concentrate on the Songhay Empire. Instead, they foolishly waged wars against each other. They were never able to unite and rule in peace. Each one tried to take a part of the empire.

This state of affairs lasted for several years. Finally, Daoud, the youngest son of Askia Mohammed, took power in 1549 C.E. He ruled until his death in 1582 C.E.

THE MOROCCAN OCCUPATION BEGINS WITH THE SALT MINES, 1590 C.E.

The Moroccans had eyed the empire for many years, and, in 1585 C.E., they successfully occupied the famous salt mines of Taghaza. By 1590 C.E. when the Moroccans invaded the empire of Songhay, it was caught up in the petty jealousies and rivalries left over from the time of rule by Askia Mohammed's sons. The Songhay Empire was now in deep decline. It was helpless against the strong invading Moroccans.

The Moroccans now took over Songhay under the leadership of the African Spaniard, Judar Pasha. He had been born in Morocco but grew up in Spain. Pasha was captured by the Moors, Africans who had accepted the religion of Islam and were committed to the conquest of Europe, when he was a teenager. The Moors had raised him in Spain, but when he turned 20 he returned to Africa and became a major figure in Moroccan history.

The Moroccans invaded with 5,000 mercenary soldiers hired from the areas of Tunisia and Algeria. The mercenaries were equipped with cannons and guns from England. They had enough provisions of food and water to last through long battles. Their "modern" weapons were far superior to the bows and arrows and spears of the Songhay soldiers. Spears and lances would prove to be no match for bullets and cannonballs.

The Moroccans devastated most of the major cities in the empire, destroying all they came across. They completely defeated the army of Songhay. However, the country was never brought to its knees and the people never accepted Moroccan rule. The people made it difficult for the Moroccans to control so vast an empire. Because the army could not patrol all areas, the smaller villages were never secured.

Most important, the Moroccans never succeeded in discovering where the Songhay gold mines were located. The Moroccans had started using the salt mines to help them trade for better, more costly goods. But they never found the gold mines. The Songhay people never cooperated with the Moroccans enough to reveal that great national secret.

The Moroccan rulers had other problems with the former Songhay kingdoms. The kingdoms kept revolting, forming small armies or groups, and attacking the Moroccan army.

These organized guerilla attacks weakened the Moroccan army because they spent so much time putting down the attacks. The Moroccans never managed to keep the peace in the large cities of the empire.

A sporadic Moroccan occupation of the Songhay Empire lasted for nearly one and a half centuries, almost 150 years. By 1740 C.E., it was all over. During this period, the whole empire that had been Songhay was destroyed. One Sudanese scholar has written:

"From that moment on, everything changed. Danger took the place of security; poverty of wealth. Peace gave way to distress, disasters and violence."

As Chancellor Williams, an African American historian, has written:

"At the beginning of the seventeenth century, the Golden Age of the western Sudan had reached its nadir."

As the curtain finally fell on the Songhay Empire, Africans were being taken from the continent to various parts of the Americas. With them went the African ideas, rhythms, religious expression, philosophies, and behaviors of the classical cultures of West Africa. The seeming swiftness of the decline of classical Africa belies the historical significance of African civilizations for the world.

1. Make a timeline of the events which led to the demise and downfall of the Songhay Empire. (You do not have to include dates, but the sequence or order should be correct.) Why were the Moroccans able to conquer Songhay?

2. Why do you think that the Moroccans failed to bring the Songhay people to their knees and completely defeat them?

3. Who or what group was really responsible for the doom of Songhay, in your opinion? Why? Is there danger today of repeating the doom of a great empire or culture? What should be done to preserve it, instead? Explain your thinking.

CHAPTER

30 ◆ SONGHAY SHATTERS INTO A THOUSAND PIECES

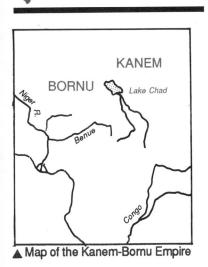

KANEM

BORNU   Lake Chad

Niger R.

Benue

Congo

▲ Map of the Kanem-Bornu Empire

THE KANEM-BORNU EMPIRE COMES TO GREATNESS, 850 C.E. TO 1800 C.E.

Before and after the Songhay Empire fell, many small African empires arose in the central Sudan. The major kingdoms were Kanem, Bornu, some states among the Hausa-Fulani, the Akan, and the Benin-Yoruba kingdoms in the west.

Several of these smaller central Sudanic empires paralleled the major empires of Ghana, Mali, and Songhay in time period, stability, and political efficiency. The Kanem-Bornu Empire would last for a thousand years from 850 C.E. to the 19th century, carrying on the tradition of great intellectual, artistic, and political contributions that were typical of the major Sudanic empires.

The metropolitan people who lived in the cities of the Kanem-Bornu kingdom were the Kanuri. Like the Mandinka, the metropolitan people of these empires produced the kings because they represented the core political and cultural power group.

The Sefuwa family was the royal family of the Kanem-Bornu Empire. They ruled the governments of Kanem-Bornu in a benevolent and kind way. The only written records of this kingdom that we have begin with the 9th century C.E. There is evidence, however, that this important empire rivaled the greatness of Ghana, Mali, and Songhay in the enlightened way that it kept law and order in a multiethnic, culturally diverse kingdom.

Kanem was a vital link between Egypt and the rest of Africa. The people of the Lake Chad region produced goods that were sent into North Africa across the desert. Metalware, kola nuts, ivory, and other goods were traded for horses and copper from the north.

THE END OF THE CLASSICAL AGE IN AFRICA, 1800 C.E.

Situated at the historic crossroads of the Sudanic belt, Kanem protected more of its past than the periphery kingdoms along the seacoasts. Yet, even the mighty interior kingdom of Kanem gave way to the colonizing adventures of Europe. Other cultures and traditions would find their way in a new African history in the 20th and 21st centuries.

The intricate bronze casting of Benin sculpture shows the refinement of African art and skill. ▼

Already in the southern, eastern, and central regions of Africa, other empires had stretched their wings and were covering vast territories. Thus, the Zimbabwe kingdom, the Rozvi kingdom, the Angola kingdom, the Congo kingdom, the Baganda kingdom, the revitalized Ethiopian Empire represented specific spheres of influence. While not included in the discussions of classical Africa, these civilizations and kingdoms demonstrate the massive human response to society, politics, religion, law, and culture inherent in the African experience. Another volume could cover the entire scope of great African empires and include the preceding kingdoms. However, it has been the purpose of this volume to discuss the classical civilizations of Africa.

Africans who now are scattered in North America, South America, the Caribbean, and Europe are the direct descendants of the various ethnic groups (Mandinka, Yoruba, Ibo, Hausa, Kanuri, and so on) of many of the Sudanic empires.

A journey through the classical cultures of Africa touches all of the fabled capitals of the eastern and western regions. The road crosses what have become universal human themes, issues, and behaviors, and will lead you to new altitudes where your attitudes are transformed.

With this book, you have taken this road; you have journeyed through a history that, possibly, you have never studied before. We started along the Nile River and ended along the Niger River, or the Joliba River. Along the way, we saw how classical African civilizations rooted in traditions of power were changed by innovative and adventurous men and women of courage.

The end of this book is not the end of the story. The Africans in the Americas and the Africans who remain on the continent of Africa are the descendants of the classical African societies and cultures described in this book.

More than 100 different African ethnic groups were brought to America. The people spoke Mande, Wolof, Twi, Hausa, Ibo, and scores of other languages. We Africans were brought to the Americas and often cut off from our classical history. Other Americans often did not know our history, either. With this book, many of us begin our personal journey to *center,* to reconnect, to relocate ourselves in the human story that begins with the ancient classical civilizations along the life-giving rivers of Africa.

CENTER YOUR THINKING

1. List some of the African empires in the central Sudan.

2. How did the Sefuwa family govern the Kanem-Bornu Empire? Do you think that benevolent rule is good or bad? Explain.

3. CRITICAL THINKING: How did European colonization affect the culture and traditions of African kingdoms such as Kanem? Explain.

UNIT REVIEW

SUMMARY

Sunni Ali Ber, the African leader, was recognized as the greatest African leader and as one of the greatest world leaders of his time by Africans and Europeans alike. Europeans called him Sunni Heli, King of Timbuktu, and said that his empire extended all the way to the Atlantic Ocean. (p.126)

Ahmed Baba was recognized as the greatest scholar of his time in the 16th century. He established a tradition of apprenticeship that is still in practice in Africa today.(p.133)

Several small, central Sudanic empires were similar to the great classical empires of Ghana, Mali, and Songhay. The Kanem-Bornu Empire, which lasted 1,000 years from 850 C.E. to the 19th century is a primary example. (p.139)

Under Emperor Askia Mohammed, the religion of Islam and African arts and culture were allowed to flourish in freedom. A new era of African culture began with the influence of Islam impacting the feelings and beliefs of the people. Many believers in traditional African culture were not encouraged, and Islam did not encourage expression in painting or sculpture. (p. 132)

As the classical age ended in Africa, Africans and their ethnic and culture diversity scattered into North America, South America, the Caribbean, and Europe. (p. 140)

Understanding history is a journey to *center* ourselves in the human journey of self-understanding, which includes understanding our history and culture in a personal way. (p. 141)

PERSONAL WITNESSING

REFLECTION

Sunni Ali Ber was committed to preserving ancient African culture and traditions. Think about why preserving culture and tradition is important to you. Make a list of your reflections on why this is important, both for the world and for you, personally.

TESTIMONY

Share in writing, song, poem, rap, dance, or another expression of your choosing, your thoughts on centering yourself in classical Africa. If you are African or African American, how has the experience of centering been a special experience? If you are not African or African American, how do you feel about centering yourself within a different culture? How do you feel about taking the experiences of a culture and making them part of *your* center and beliefs?

GLOSSARY

administrative (ad-MIH-nih-stray-tiv) supervisory; managerial

afterlife (AF-ter-lyf) life after death

ancestor (AN-ses-ter) one from whom a person is descended, such as a great grandparent

annex (AN-neks) to add on to one's property or kingdom

artifact (ARE-tuh-fakt) something, usually useful, created by humans that is a remnant of an earlier historical period; pottery, tools, and cave paintings are examples

assembly (ah-SEM-blee) a gathering of people for a particular purpose

astronomy (ah-STRAH-noh-mee) the study of matter and objects that are outside the Earth's atmosphere

avenue (AV-eh-nyoo) a route to somewhere or to something

bureaucracy (byoo-RAH-kruh-see) a policy-making group that manages or supervises a state or other body of people

Brilliant (BRIL-yant) the stage or period during which an empire's power and culture explode into greatness

cabinet (CAH-buh-net) a group of advisors to a head of state

cadi (kah-DEE) a supreme judge in Mansa Musa's government in Mali, who handed down decisions and dispensed justice

calendar (CAH-len-der) a system for dividing the year into months, weeks, days, and so forth, all in a definite order; based on the number of days needed for the Earth to go around the sun; the ancient Egyptians developed the calendar we use today

capitulation (kah-PIH-tyoo-lay-shen) the act of yielding or surrendering, usually after negotiating terms

caste (KAST) the class of society into which a person is born

catalog (KAH-tuh-log) a list of items

cataract-(KAH-tuh-rakt) areas where rocks jut out of a river to form rapids and to create dangerous waterfalls

character (KAR-ik-ter) a feature or quality that distinguishes or makes up the personality of a person, a people, or a country

chariot (CHAR-ee-ut) a ceremonial military carriage

charismatic (kah-riz-MAH-tik) having a special personal magnetic charm or appeal that arouses great popular loyalty

civilization (sih-vih-lih-ZAY-shen) a culture with a very high level of thought, manners, and taste; sophisticated written and oral records develop

classical (CLAH-sih-kul) standard, traditional; in Chapter 1 of this text, classical refers to periods or seasons; during each classical season, major ideas, art forms, and attitudes grew in Africa

coastline (KOHST-lyn) an imaginary line that forms a boundary between the land and an ocean or a lake

colonize (KAH-luh-nyz) to establish a settlement of inhabitants

colonnade (KOH-leh-nayd) a series of stone columns set at regular intervals, usually supporting the base of a roof

commerce (KAH-mers) the trading or buying and selling of things on a large scale that involves transportation from place to place

commodity (kah-MAH-dih-tee) any product produced by people by manufacturing, mining, and the like

complex (KOM-pleks) something made up of complicated or interrelated parts; in Chapter 5 of this text, a house made up of many different rooms that are related to each other by style, colors, or other characteristics

complexion (kum-PLEK-shen) skin tone; shade of color

conquest (KAHN-kwest) gaining or taking by force; defeat

contemporary (kon-TEM-poh-reh-ree) modern; up-to-date; current

continent (KON-tih-nent) a large, continuous mass of land

control (kun-TROHL) to have power over someone, something, or a situation; to regulate

controversy (KAHN-truh-ver-see) a discussion of opposing views; a dispute; an argument

convert (kun-VERT) to bring over from one belief or view to another creation (kree-AY-shen) the act of bringing something in this text, the world into existence

crossroads (KROS-rohdz) a meeting place of importance

Dawning (DAW-neeng) a stage or period that signifies the rise of an empire

decentralize (dee-SEN-truh-lyz) to distribute power of government among those in position to assist a ruler

descendant (dih-SEN-dent) a child, grandchild, and so forth, of a person

desert (DEH-zert) an arid, barren land, usually incapable of supporting human life without a water supply that is provided by artificial means

dialect (DY-uh-lekt) a regional or local version of a major language

dignity (DIG-nih-tee) the quality or state of being worthy, honored, or esteemed

diplomacy (di-PLOH-muh-see) the art of saying the right thing at the right time in order to get people to come to agreement

Drought (DROWT) a period of dryness that causes great damage to crops; in Egypt, the season from February to June when the Nile's water level is very low

duality (doo-AH-luh-tee) opposite forces within the same being

duba (DOO-buh) a massive drum made from a long, hollow tree trunk and used to call the people together

dynasty (DY-nuh-stee) a ruling family

Emergence (ee-MER-jens) the season in Egypt when the waters of the Nile match their peak in September and begin to recede

enslaved (en-SLAYVD) forced into slavery

eternal (ee-TER-nul) never ending

ethnology (eth-NAH-loh-gee) a study that analyzes and compares different cultures

expansive (ek-SPAN-siv) sizable; extensive

flesh (flesh) human; in Chapter 17, Manicheans believe that "all flesh is evil" everything human is evil and only the spirit is pure

foundation (fown-DAY-shen) the basis of something

gateway (GAYT-way) a key position or location that leads to many places and things

generosity (jeh-neh-RAH-sih-tee) the quality of freely giving of oneself or of one's wealth

geometry (jee-AH-meh-tree) a branch of math that deals with the measurement and relationships of angles, solids, lines, and surfaces; developed by ancient Africans, it was used by Egyptians to measure land and to settle boundary disputes

Glowing (GLO-eeng) the stage or period during which an empire comes into its own strength

god (gahd) a being or object said to have supernatural power, control a particular aspect of life, and require humans to worship it

guerilla (guh-REE-ya) a person or group of people who engage in irregular warfare, especially using sabotage and harassment

hierarchical (hy-uh-RAR-kih-kul) related to a ruling body that is organized into ranks, each one answering to the one above it

hieroglyphics (hy-roh-FLIH-fiks) ancient Egyptian writings that were a mixture of pictograms, signs, symbols, and syllables

highlands (HI-landz) elevated or mountainous areas of land

indentured (in-DEN-tyoord) a type of servant who works for another person for a period of time to pay off a debt

indigenous (in-DIH-jih-nis) native-born people of a region, or something produced or grown in a region

inflation (in-FLAY-shen) a period when prices are high or rising above where they should be so that your money buys less and, therefore, is worth less

ingenious (in-JEEN-yus) showing intelligence and skill at discovering, inventing, or planning a way to handle a situation

inherent (in-HEHR-ent) belonging to something by nature or habit; involved in the essential character of something; for example, germs are inherent in a virus

inscription (in-SKRIP-shen) something that is written, engraved, or imprinted

interior (in-TEE-ree-ur) land area lying away from a border, shore, or other boundary intermediary (in-tur-MEE-dee-eh-ree) a person or power acting as a go-between for both sides of a dispute

Inundation (in-un-DAY-shen) the period in Egypt from June to September when the Nile's waters overflow its banks

jihad (JEE-had) Islamic religious wars

ka (KAH) a body preserved for life after-death

legacy (LEH-guh-see) a gift from an ancestor or a ruler to a person, a people, or a nation; in modern day, it is usually left in a will to someone; for example, by their early achievements, inventions, and discoveries, the ancient Africans left a legacy of knowledge for all people

lifestyle (LYF styl) the typical way of life of a person, a group, or a culture

mastaba (MAS-tuh-buh) boxlike tombs used as resting places before the pyramids became burial places

matrilineal (mah-truh-LIH-nee-ul) when the power to rule is passed through the female line in the family; Chapter 13 tells that royal power in Nubia was passed form the dead ruler to the child of the dead ruler's sister

medu neter (MEH-doo NAY-tur) the language of ancient Africa

model (MAH-duh) a standard or guide for people to follow or to try to copy

monarchy (MAH-nar-kee) royal leadership

monolith (MAH-noh-lith) a single massive stone, often in the form of a column or an obelisk

mosque (MOSK) a place of worship for Muslims, or believers in the Islamic religion

motif (moh-TEEF) a design, plan, symbol, or theme

multicultural (mul-tee-KUL-tyoo-rul) of many different cultures

multiethnic (mul-tee-ETH-nik) of many different racial, tribal, religious, or other groups

mummy (MUH-mee) a preserved dead body

myth (MITH) a story usually about a god or national hero

nadir (NAY-deer) the bottom; the lowest point

narrative (NAH-ruh-tiv) a story that is told

natron (NAY-trahn) a chemical used for embalming, or preserving, a dead body before it is wrapped during the process of mummification

natural resource (NAH-tyoo-rul REE-sors) a material, such as a mineral or waterpower, supplied by nature that can be used in industry

noble (NOH-bul) a person of high birth, social rank, or government position

nomad (NOH-mad) one who does not settle in one place but moves from place to place

obelisk (AH-bul-isk) a tall four-sided pillar that tapers as it rises to a small pyramid at its top; usually built in praise of the gods

occupation (ah-kyoo-PAY-shen) the holding and control of an area or country by a foreign military force

omnipresence (OM-nee-preh-zens) being present in all ways, all places, all the time; controlling all the opposing forces and keeping them in harmony and unity

oracle (AW-rah-kul) a place where, or a person through whom, a god speaks

ostrakon (OS-trah-kon) a piece of broken pottery with either designs or writing on the outside

papyrus (puh-PY-ris) lightweight writing paper made from the papyrus plant; the first form of paper, it was made in Kemet

paramount (PAR-uh-mownt) superior to all others

patriarchal (pay-tree-ARE-kul) of a government that is ruled by males

pavilion (puh-VIL-yin) a large, often rich-looking tent

pharaoh (fay-ROH) usually, a king of Egypt; when Hatshepsut became the first woman pharaoh of Egypt, she insisted on being called "king"

pictogram (PIK-toh-gram) a picture that stands for words or letters

pilgrimage (PIL-grim-ij) a journey especially to a shrine or sacred religious place

placate (PLAY-kayt) to soothe or keep happy by making concessions; to appease; to pacify

precaution (pre-KAW-shen) care taken in advance to prevent harm or to secure good

prehistoric (pree-his-TAW-rik) a period of which there is no written language

principle (PRIN-sih-pul) a basic law, belief, or assumption

priority (pry-AH-rih-tee) superiority in rank, position, or importance that places something or someone over another

procession (proh-SEH-shen) a group of people walking as part of a ceremony

protectorate (proh-TEK-toh-rayt) a territory under the political control of another state or empire

pylon (PY-lun) a giant wall of stone, usually built near a temple

pyramid (PIR-uh-mid) a giant structure; four stone triangles whose points meet at the top; used as tombs by ancient Egyptian royalty

reserve (ree-ZURV) something set aside for a particular purpose; in the economic sense, gold or money that is kept out of circulation to avoid inflation; an amount of cash, for example, that has been put aside until really needed for hard times

resettlement (ree-SET-tul-ment) euphemism for the removal of a people to another area in which they are forced to live

Rosetta stone (roh-ZET-tuh stohn) a solid black slab; translating the message on it gave scholars sthe key to ancient Egyptian writing

sahel (sah-HEL) a dry, semidesert region

savanna (suh-VAH-nuh) a treeless, grassy plain

scholar (SKAH-lur) one who attends a school or who studies under a teacher

scribe (SKRYB) an honored official who was given the task of writing down all the important events

sesh (SEHSH) scribes of ancient Egypt

security (see-KYOO-ruh-tee) safety

shawabti (shah-WAB-tee) a statuette made for a funeral and placed in the tomb to serve the dead person in the afterlife

siege (SEEJ) a continual, serious attack to force complete surrender

silt (SILT) fertile soil, usually in the form of mud and usually on the banks of a river, that allows agriculture to take place

sphinx (SFEENKS) a giant Egyptian statue usually with a woman's head and a lion's body; myth said that the sphinx would kill anyone who was unable to answer the riddle it asked

stela (STEH-lah) a stone slab or pillar built to honor a god or royalty

strategist (STRAH-tih-jist) a person who is especially skillful at making plans toward achieving a goal

subject (SUB-jekt) under the authority or control of someone or something else

subjugate (SUB-joo-gayt) to conquer; to bring under control; to subdue; to make submissive

supply (suh-PLY) a needed or available amount of money, gold or food and the like

supremacy (soo-PREH-muh-see) the quality of being the highest in authority or power

theology (thee-AH-luh-jee) the study of a god or gods and their relation to the world

totem (TOH-tum) the use of an animal or something in nature to symbolize, or represent, certain cultural beliefs

tradition (truh-DIH-shen) an established pattern of thought, action, or behavior that people have inherited or follow by custom

traditional (truh-DIH-shen-ul) having to do with an established pattern of thought, action, or behavior that people have inherited or follow by custom

tropical (TRH-pih-kul) describes a frost-free area with temperatures high enough for year-round plant growth, given sufficient moisture

unity (YOO-nih-tee) oneness

vassal (VAH-sul) a person or state that owes its protection to another person or nation

villa (VIH-lah) a rural or country estate, usually the residence of a wealthy person

vizier (vuh-ZEER) a prime minister; second in importance, responsibility, and power to the king

wane (WAYN) diminish; lessen; decline

worship (WUR-ship) honor that is offered to a divine being or a god; to respect or honor a divine being or supernatural power

Abu Simbel (ah-boo SIHM-bul) site of two rock temples of Ramses II (built around 1250 B.C.E.

Abydos (ah-BID-is) ancient town on the Nile in southern Egypt, south of Thebes

Adulis (AH-dyoo-lis) the multicultural and multiethnic symbol of Axum's political importance, this city along with Yeha (YAY-hah) and Kaskase (KAHS-kayz) in its earlier years, became a center of influence and trade up and down the Red Sea between Axum and Egypt; later because of its location as a seaport, it became Axum's gateway to the world

Akhenaten (ah-ken-AH-ten) name chosen by Egyptian pharaoh Amenhotep IV (circa 14th century B.C.E.)

Allah (AH-lah) Islamic; the Almighty God

Al-Bakri (ahl-BAH-ree) Writer who provides much in his works of the history and culture of Ghana

Almoravids (ahl-meh-RAH-vihdz) warriors of the Berber ethnic group of peoples; invaded and overthrew the rulers of the Ghanaian Empire in the 11th century C.E. and forced the acceptance both of Islam as the empire's religion and of the change to Arabic names for the people; their rule lasted 50 years

Amanitore (ah-MAH-nih-tawr) powerful Kushite queen (25-41 C.E.)

Amen (AH-men) Egyptian: called "the hidden;" the great sun god of the city of Thebes and one of the supreme gods in ancient Egypt; his temple at Karnak is a great architectural achievement

Asclepios (az-klep-AY-uz) Greek god of medicine who, in real life, was the Egyptian Imhotep, who laid the foundations for the study and practice of medicine

Askia Mohammed (ahs-KEE-ah moh-HAH-med) Songhay emperor (circa 1530's C.E.) under whom the religion of Islam and African arts and culture were allowed to flourish in freedom; his use of a cabinet of advisors made him the first modern ruler of what is today Sudan

Aspelta (ah-SPEHL-tah) wealthy and powerful Nubian king from 600 B.C.E. to 580 B.C.E. whose armies were eventually defeated by the Egyptians and forced to withdraw from Napata to Meroe

Assyria (ah-SEE-ree-ah) Asian country, now Iraq, that defeated the combined armies of Egypt and Nubia in 660 B.C.E. to control the Nile Valley; this led to the eventual end of the kingdom of Kush

Aswan (AH-swahn) Egyptian city on the right bank of the Nile; in 1970, the Egyptian government built the Aswan High Dam there to control the floodwaters of the Nile and to provide irrigation for farmland

Aten (AH-tun) a minor sun god who was elevated to supreme and the only god briefly by Pharaoh Amenhotep IV, who even changed his name to Akenhaten in honor of Aten

Atum (AH-toom) Egyptian: called "the Almighty;" one of the supreme sun gods in ancient Egypt; worshiped in the city of Heliopolis

Audoghast (AW doh-gahst) the city that was the salt capital of the Ghanaian Empire

Axum (AHK-soom) capital of ancient Ethiopian kingdom known as the Axumite Empire; a great center of commerce and power politics, a powerfully artistic civilization, a forceful military power, and a religious center which contained, according to tradition, the Ark of the Covenant, brought from Jerusalem by a descendant of Solomon and the Queen of Sheba

Cleopatra (klee-oh-PAH-trah) Egyptian queen of Greek descent who surrendered control of Egypt to Rome (69-30 B.C.E.)

Champollion, Jean (shahm-pole-YOHN, ZHAHN) French translator of the Rosetta Stone, providing the key to the ancient Egyptian hieroglyphics

Ezana I (ay-ZAH-nah the first) king of the region of Axum in the 4th century C.E.; conquered the Beja nation; assisted in the conversion of much of the area to Christianity

Ghana (GAH-nah) earliest of the ancient empires of the Sudan in West Africa in what is now Mali and parts of Senegal, Guinea, Morocco, and Mauretania; first called Wagadu (modern Oagadougou); known as the kingdom of ivory and gold; also, the king of Ghana

Hapi (HOP-ee) god of the Nile River

Hathor (HAT-hor) Egyptian goddess of health and prosperity

Hatshepsut (hat-SHEP-soot) first woman pharaoh of Egypt; also known as Ma'at Ka Re; built many obelisks and stelae to praise the gods; sent explorers and traders to the east coast of Africa (16th - 15th century B.C.E.)

Heliodorus (hee-lee-oh-DOH-rus) Greek who wrote the important novel *Aethiopica,* a good source about the Axumite Empire

Heliopolis (hee-lee-AH-poh-lis) ancient holy city in Lower Egypt dedicated to worship of the god Atum and the sun god Ra; two of its most famed obelisks were called Cleopatra's Needles

Herodotus (heh-roh-DOH-tus) famous Greek philosopher who stated that Egypt is the home of the name of nearly all the gods

Homer (HOH-muhr) Greek epic poet who studied ancient Egyptian history and culture

Horus (HO-russ) Egyptian god of the sky; the "living ruler"

Islam (IHS-lahm) the religious faith of the Arabs; belief includes in Allah as the only god as Mohammed as his prophet; followers of this religion are called Muslims

Imhotep (im-HOH-tep) 28th. century B.C.E. vizier (prime minister) of Egypt; architect who built the Step Pyramid at Sakkara, the first pyramid used as a king's tomb; discovered the source of the Blue Nile in Nubia; worshiped as a god of medicine because of his advances

Isis (EYE-siz) Egyptian mother goddess and protector of the dead, wife of Osiris and mother of Horus

Isocrates (ih-SAHK-ruh-teez) Greek orator who studied ancient Egyptian culture and history

Kagemni (kah-JEHM-nee) great African teacher during the second classical season (525-641 C.E.)

Karnak (KAR-nahk) north part of ancient Thebes; site of many temples, including prehistoric one of Amen and those by Amenhotep III, Seti I, and Ramses II

Kemet (keh-MET) the African name of ancient Egypt before the Greeks changed it to Aigyptos (i-GIP tos)

Khafre (KAH-fray) 26th century B.C.E. king of Egypt and son of King Khufu; erected the second-largest pyramid in Egypt, near his father's at Giza

Khartoum (kar-TOOM) city of Sudan at the junction of the White Nile and Blue Nile rivers

Khnum (kuh-NOOM) Egyptian: called "the Creator;" god of the source of the Nile

Khufu (KOO-foo) also known by the Greek name

Cheops (KEE-ops) 26th century B.C.E. king of Egypt; erected the Great Pyramid at Giza around 2644 B.C.E., one of the Seven Wonders of the Ancient World

Khun-anup (KOON uh-NOOP) great African teacher during the second classical season (525-641 C.E.)

Koran -koh-RAHN) sacred book of the Islamic religion

Kumbi (KOOM-bee) capital city and gold center of the Ghanaian Empire

Kush (KOOSH) ancient country in the Nile valley adjoining Egypt; one of the two great parts of the Nubian kingdom

Luxor (LUHK-sawr) southern part of ancient Theban site of temples by Amhotep III, Ikhnaton, and Ramses II

Mali (MAH-lee) West African empire in the West Sahara and Sudan regions; important landmarks are the River Niger and Timbuktu; rose under Sundiata Keita from almost nothing to the largest, richest, most organized empire in West Africa; Sundiata left the foundation for it to become a civilization unparalleled in West Africa

Mansa Musa (MAN-sah moo-SAH) descendant of Sundiata Keita and emperor of Mali around the early 1330's C.E.; conquered the Songhay Empire, expanded trade, and supported education and the arts

medu neter (MEH-doo NAY-tur) the language of ancient Africa

Memphis (MEHM-fihs) ancient city of Lower Egypt and traditionally the capital of both Menes and most Egyptian rulers through the 18th dynasty; lost its importance after Alexander the Great conquered Egypt; sacred to the worship of Ptah

Menes (MEE-neez) first pharaoh of Egypt; founder of the first dynasty about 3100 B.C.E.; also known as Narmer (circa 31st century B.C.E.)

Menkaure (mehn-kah-OO-ray) 26th century B.C.E. king of Egypt and son of King Khafre; erected the third-largest pyramid in Egypt, near his father's; it is the most perfectly built pyramid of the three at Giza

Meroe (MEH-roh-way) ancient city on the east bank of the Nile; capital of Ethiopian kings from about 750 B.C.E. and of Nubia from 500 B.C.E. to 300 B.C.E.; one of the two great parts of the Nubian kingdom

Mohammed (moh-HAH-med) Arab prophet, circa 570-632 C.E., and founder of the religion of Islam

Napata (NAH-pah-tah) Kushite city that was the first great capital of Nubia

Natakamani (NAH-tah-kah-MAH-nee) husband and chief advisor to Queen Amanitore

Nkrumah, Kwame (ehn-KROO-mah, KWAH-mee) (1909-1972) Ghanaian politician who led the Gold Coast in its successful fight for freedom from British rule; first president of the Ghana republic (1960-1966); called the modern father of Ghana

Nubia, Nubian (NOO-bee-ah, NOO-bee-en) the oldest civilization about which we know, in the area of Egypt today; an Egyptian who has very black skin

Osiris (oh-Sy-rus) Egyptian god of the afterworld, death, rebirth, and agriculture

Persia (PER-zhuh) Asian empire that invaded Egypt during the second classical season (525-641 C.E.) to gain Egyptian ideas, advances, and knowledge; today, Persia is known as the republic of Iran

Piankhi (PYAN-kee) Nubian king who led the first recorded conquest of Egypt and reigned as pharaoh of a combined egypt and Nubia (8th century B.C.E.); erected granite stelae in both areas and revived the study of Nubian culture in Egypt

Plato (PLAY-toh) Greek philosopher who studied ancient Egyptian culture and history

Ptah (puh-TAH) Egyptian: called "the Almighty;" one of the supreme sun gods in ancient Egypt; worshiped in the city of Memphis

Punt (POONT) ancient Egyptian name for what is now part of the coast of Somalia; visit by Pharaoh Hatshepsut in the 13th century B.C.E. established trade with Egypt of Punt's myrrh, gold, ebony, incense, animals, and fruit

Pythagoras (pih-THAH-goh-ruhs) Greek philosopher and mathematician who studied Egyptian history and culture; made great advances in math and astronomy as a result of this

Ra (RAH) Egyptian: called "the Almighty;" one of the supreme sun gods in ancient Egypt; worshiped in the city of Heliopolis

Ramses II (RAM-sees) pharaoh whose reign (1304-1237 B.C.E.) was the last peak of Egyptian imperial power; completed the temple at Abydos, built great mortuary temple at Thebes and the rock-cut temple at Abu Simbel, as well as temples at Karnak and Luxor

Senmut (SEHN-moot) architect who built the temple/tomb of Hatshepsut in the Valley of the Queens near the modern city of Luxor

Snefru (SNEH-froo) 27th-26th century B.C.E. king of Egypt and father of Khufu; erected what is considered the third-largest but first true pyramid in Egypt at Dahshur (dah-SHOOR); pyramid is called the Crooked Pyramid because of bulges in its sides; brought Egypt to a high level of prosperity; raided Nubia, conquered Sinai, and developed copper mines

Somalia (soh-MAH-lee-ah) semidesert country of East Africa, later under the protectorate of Britain and, even later, Italy; now a republic

Sonchis (SAHN-kihs) great African teacher during the second classical season (525-641 C.E.)

Songhay (sohg-HY) empire region in the bend of the Niger River in west central Sudan; last great kingdom of West Africa; its city of Djenne (DYEHN) was the home of its extremely advanced culture, education, arts, and sciences

Sumanguru (SOO-man-goo-roo) Ghanaian king hwo defeated the Mallinke king and added Malli to his kingdom (13th century C.E.)

Sundiata Keita (soon-JAH-tah KAY-tah) founder and first king of the Mali Empire (around 1255 C.E.)

Sunni Ali Ber (SOO-nee AH-lee BER) Emperor of Songhay (late 15th century C.E.); reestablished the presence of African culture in religion, education, and traditions

Syria (SEE-ree-ah) ancient region of Asia bordering on the Mediterranean and covering modern Syria, Lebanon, Israel, and Jordan; while Syria invaded ancient Egypt, it was conquered by the Egyptians

Taharka (tuh-HAR-kuh) pharaoh of Egypt; Nubian king (689-664 B.C.E.) who defeated the invading Assyrians to defend his ally, Israel; mentioned in the Bible in both the books of Isaish and Kings; revived and fostered cultural life, new building and restoration of old ones; his tomb held more than a thousand *shawabtis*

Tehuti (teh-HOO-tee) Egyptian: god of literature and knowledge; taught people how to write and showed them what to write; also called Thoth

Thebes (THEEBZ) an ancient capital city of Egypt, center for the worship of the god Amen

Tutankhamen (too-tan-KAH-man) pharaoh of Egypt who lived around 1370-1352 B.C.E.; son of Amenhotep III; much of his reign was controlled by advisors, but he did return to the African religion of Amen and moved the capital again to Memphis from Thebes; his tomb was discovered in 1922 C.E. in the Valley of the Kings

Wennofer (WEHN-nuh-fuhr) great African teacher and scholar during the second classical season (525-641 C.E.)

Zoser (ZHO-zur) Egyptian pharaoh who had Imhotep build the Step Pyramid at Sakkara in about 2800 B.C.E.; this was the first pyramid to be used as a king's tomb